First Steps in
SAP® Controlling (CO)

Ashish Sampat

Thank you for purchasing this book from Espresso Tutorials!

Like a cup of espresso coffee, Espresso Tutorials SAP books are concise and effective. We know that your time is valuable and we deliver information in a succinct and straightforward manner. It only takes our readers a short amount of time to consume SAP concepts. Our books are well recognized in the industry for leveraging tutorial-style instruction and videos to show you step by step how to successfully work with SAP.

Check out our YouTube channel to watch our videos at
https://www.youtube.com/user/EspressoTutorials.

If you are interested in SAP Finance and Controlling, join us at
http://www.fico-forum.com/forum2/
to get your SAP questions answered and contribute to discussions.

Related titles from Espresso Tutorials:

► Sydnie McConnell & Martin Munzel: First Steps in SAP® (2nd, extended edition)
   http://5045.espresso-tutorials.com

► Martin Munzel: New SAP® Controlling Planning Interface
   http://5011.espresso-tutorials.com

► Michael Esser: Investment Project Controlling with SAP®
   http://5008.espresso-tutorials.com

► Stefan Eifler: Quick Guide to SAP® CO-PA (Profitability Analysis)
   http://5018.espresso-tutorials.com

► Paul Ovigele: Reconciling SAP® CO-PA to the General Ledger
   http://5040.espresso-tutorials.com

► Tanya Duncan: Practical Guide to SAP® CO-PC (Product Cost Controlling)
   http://5064.espresso-tutorials.com

► Janet Salmon & Ulrich Schlüter: SAP® HANA for ERP Financials, 2nd edition
   http://5092.espresso-tutorials.com

► Ann Cacciottolli: First Steps in SAP® Financial Accounting (FI)
   http://5095.espresso-tutorials.com

Ashish Sampat
First Steps in SAP® Controlling (CO)

ISBN:　　　　　978-1-5170-3270-8

Editor:　　　　Alice Adams

Proofreading:　Lisa Jackson

Cover Design:　Philip Esch, Martin Munzel

Cover Photo:　　istockphoto # 13841366 (c) YanLev

Interior Design: Johann-Christian Hanke

All rights reserved.

1st Edition 2015, Gleichen

© 2015 by Espresso Tutorials GmbH

URL: *www.espresso-tutorials.com*

Feedback
We greatly appreciate any kind of feedback you have concerning this book. Please mail us at *info@espresso-tutorials.com*.

Table of Contents

Acknowledgements

A number of years back, a colleague introduced me to a book called *The Goal: A Process of Ongoing Improvement* by Eliyahu M. Goldratt. The best-selling business novel explained the theory of constraints in an easy to understand story form. I was awed by the simple explanation of a very complex topic. I read the book several times and my admiration for the author grew each time.

Recently, while I was providing an overview of a client's SAP design to a fellow consultant, he suddenly asked me if I was going to write a book on SAP. I was taken aback for a while and thought to myself, well, it is not a bad idea. I decided I would wait for the right opportunity to take up this project.

Opportunity knocked the door when the Espresso Tutorials' team reached out regarding a potential book project. There are very few books that introduce SAP Controlling and we thought that readers could benefit from a book on this topic. While working on the book outline, I thought of the idea of following the format used in *The Goal*. This book is seen through the eyes of Alex — a finance professional who is learning his new job as a plant cost analyst at Global Confectioners, Inc.

I want to thank the team at Espresso Tutorials — particularly Martin Munzel for giving me an opportunity to write this book; and Alice Adams who painstakingly and patiently edited the book while continuously encouraging me to incorporate formatting and content suggestions.

I also want to thank my family, friends, colleagues, and fellow SAP consultants for providing continuous encouragement and support while I wrote this book. Particularly my wife, Meenal, and our children, Megha and Jash, who were supportive of me spending time completing the manuscript.

I enjoyed writing this book and I hope that you enjoy reading it.

Preface

The integrated nature of SAP business software becomes easier to comprehend when one understands the intricacies of SAP Controlling. This book is intended for beginners who would like to get an overview of the SAP Controlling module.

Set in the backdrop of Global Confectioners, Inc. (GCI) — a fictional chocolate manufacturing company — and its Chocotown manufacturing facility, this book takes the reader through several day-in-a-life scenarios of various key functions: plant finance, manufacturing, inventory control, and information systems. Seen through the eyes of Alex, who is learning his new job as Plant Cost Analyst at GCI Chocotown, the reader is introduced to SAP Controlling concepts with different examples identified from this plot. Alex learns something new every day with the help of his manager, as well as his colleagues at GCI.

This book explains some of the complex SAP Controlling concepts using a case study approach. Characters in the plot interact through dialogue and questions, concepts are explained using examples from the issue that the team is dealing with.

This book is an ideal read for anyone who wants to understand the SAP Controlling module and its integration with other modules. Whether you are new to an organization using SAP business software, a member of an SAP implementation team, or are a finance professional who simply wants to learn about SAP business software, this book will provide answers to many of your questions. Additionally, screenshots are provided with examples so that you are able to effectively visualize the data flow.

We have added a few icons to highlight important information. These include:

Tips

Tips highlight information concerning more details about the subject being described and/or additional background information.

Examples

Examples help illustrate a topic better by relating it to real world scenarios.

Attention

Attention notices draw attention to information that you should be aware of when you go through the examples from this book on your own.

Finally, a note concerning the copyright: all screenshots printed in this book are the copyright of SAP SE. All rights are reserved by SAP SE. Copyright pertains to all SAP images in this publication. For simplification, we will not mention this specifically underneath every screenshot.

1 The characters: Who's who at GCI?

Global Confectioners, Inc. (GCI) is a fictional organization that manufactures chocolates and other confectionery products. We will use GCI as a case study to walk you through real-life scenarios using SAP Controlling at a manufacturing facility. Like any other manufacturing organization, GCI has a finance controller (sometimes also referred as cost controller, or simply a controller), manufacturing manager, inventory controller, and onsite IT support staff. This book is written through the eyes of Alex, a plant cost analyst who has recently joined GCI. Alex has never used SAP software before and is an ideal candidate to take this journey with you, the reader.

1.1 Alex—Plant cost analyst at GCI

"Welcome to Global Confectioners, Inc.," Iris, the Human Resources manager, greeted Alex. Alex met Iris during the interview and hiring process and was somewhat familiar with her.

Alex was excited to start his new job as the Plant Cost Analyst for GCI at their manufacturing facility in Chocotown. For the past two years, Alex worked for Fork-o-Lift Works (FLW) in a similar role. The difference between the companies is that GCI is in a process-based industry, whereas FLW was in the discrete manufacturing industry. Alex was eager to learn more about this industry and looked forward to new career challenges.

Alex joined FLW fresh out of college. The last two years were full of on-the-job learning. A plant cost analyst is not necessarily a number cruncher, but it is important the person understands the systems and financial business processes an organization uses. People are an integral part of processes and systems and it is not only important to know who is who, but it is important to know who does what.

"First, let's go through some HR documentation and then I will introduce you to your manager, Bob," Iris said. Luckily, Alex remembered to bring his required documents to complete the necessary paperwork. Everything looked pretty similar to the paperwork he completed at FLW—just a different company name and logo. "Hopefully things will get more interesting from here," Alex thought.

"Okay, Alex, now that the paperwork is done, why don't I walk you over to Bob's office and he will take over from here," Iris said. Once at Bob's office, Iris said, "Please do not hesitate to contact me if you have any issues or concerns."

"Sure, thank you," Alex said.

1.2   Bob—Plant controller and Alex's manager at CGI

"I am so glad you are here!" said Bob. "We are so happy that we found a bright person like you to join our team."

Alex took notes as Bob explained the department structure and Alex's roles and responsibilities.

"Soon, we will start our annual budget planning process and I want you to know the ins and outs of last year's budget. Here is the file that your predecessor, Kevin, prepared. Please go over it and let me know what questions you have." Bob pointed to a bulky binder. "Have you worked with SAP software before?" Bob asked.

"No," Alex said, "we had a home-grown system at my previous employer—FLW. But I have heard a lot about SAP from other friends and colleagues who have worked with SAP and I am excited to learn more about it."

"Don't worry," Bob said. "Go through this training manual that our IT team put together. There is a lot of interesting information here. It will provide a good overview of the system setup. Going over this material should keep you busy for the next three or four days. In the meantime, we will arrange for you to get access to the system."

Alex was curious and wondered what kind of training manual took three or four days to read through. It better be detailed with examples, he thought, otherwise one could easily lose interest.

Bob continued, "We have recently been having some issues with our monthly process order reporting. The numbers that we report do not match what the manufacturing team reports. I want you to get involved with this issue as soon as you can. Another area of immediate focus for you will be to address the inventory valuation questions that the inventory control folks have."

Alex replied, "Sure, I will do my best."

"Come on, let me introduce you to the team." Bob stood up and walked towards the door.

Alex could smell cocoa as soon as they entered the manufacturing floor where chocolate was being produced. He looked forward to meeting the team.

1.3   Carl—Manufacturing manager at CGI

"Alex, meet Carl. He is responsible for manufacturing and will be your first point of contact for any questions that you have in terms of production. Carl, Alex is replacing Kevin and will be handling any costing-related queries that you have."

"Welcome, Alex. It's nice to meet you. I look forward to working with you." Carl shook hands with Alex.

To Carl, Bob said, "I am yet to look at your question on process order variances from yesterday, but will get back to you shortly."

"No worries, Bob, I understand," Carl said. "We are adding a new line next month and I will be tied up over the next few weeks, so I won't have much time to address the routine queries myself, but we will figure it out. In fact, I have a meeting with a couple of vendors and need to head off to meet them, I'll see you folks later." Carl exited his office and Alex and Bob stepped out as well.

1.4   Dave—Inventory controller at CGI

"This is our receiving and raw material storage area," Bob said. "As you can see, this is the starting point for our plant's operations. I'd like to introduce you to Dave who is responsible for this area."

Alex took a visual survey of all the drums, pallets, bins, and racks around him.

"Dave, I want you to meet Alex—he just joined today as our new plant cost analyst," Bob said.

"Oh yes, in Kevin's place, correct?" Dave said. "We have been expecting you. Welcome to GCI. My team and I were actually looking at an inventory report earlier and had a couple of questions on the valuation. Maybe once you settle in and familiarize yourself you can help us out with that. In the meantime, I'll have to pick Bob's brain."

1.5 Erin—Finance IT support at CGI

"Alex, all the people that you have met so far today are all cross-functional team members," Bob said. "However, the person whom I will introduce you to next is kind of an extension of our finance function."

"Erin, this is Alex. He just joined my team today. I have asked him to go through our finance training manual which I know you were involved with developing. Alex, this is Erin, she is very knowledgeable on our overall SAP system setup, particularly in the areas of finance and costing. I consider Erin a great asset to our IT support organization. She is often my go-to person and I bet she will be yours too."

"Uh oh," Erin said. "You exaggerate a lot, Bob. Welcome, Alex. I look forward to working with you. As Bob said, please go over the training material and let me know what questions you have."

"Nice meeting you, thanks for your help," Alex said.

What a day, Alex thought. I have to get up to speed quickly and help the team address all of these questions.

2 Controlling: What are we trying to control after all?

> "He who controls others may be powerful, but he who
> has mastered himself is mightier still."
> —Lao Tzu

The term *control* can be defined as the process of channeling efforts in a particular direction, towards a particular goal. It also includes course correction as necessary to reach the defined goal. In the context of this book, *control* refers to cost controlling, particularly in SAP Enterprise Resource Planning (ERP). In this chapter, we will look at which modules and functional areas are typically used in a manufacturing organization that uses SAP software as its system of record.

2.1 Overview of controlling

Alex sat down and opened the Finance Training Manual. He looked forward to learning about the SAP software. Alex started reading. The manual provided an overview of the SAP software system and how GCI recognized the value in streamlining processes by implementing SAP. Several pages provided step-by-step instructions on how to log into the SAP system. Alex would have to wait until he got access to GCI's system in order to try the steps out himself, but he could review the training manual until then.

The manual went into further detail on the various modules in SAP. Alex started taking notes.

2.1.1 SAP modules

Materials Management (MM)

Starting with procuring materials for the organization via a purchase order, *materials management* also deals with the movement of materials within and between various departments. MM supplies raw materials and other components for production. Once products are produced, the software enables stocking the materials in the warehouse, ready to ship when there is a need. The SAP software records a financial transaction (most of the time) when goods are moved into/within/outside the organization. Vendors submit invoices and are paid at a later date (depending on the payment terms), thereby completing the *procure-to-pay* cycle. Alex recalled that they called it a source-to-pay cycle at FLW.

Production Planning (PP)

Production planning through the materials requirement planning (MRP) functionality uses information from sales orders, demand forecasting, and available inventory in order to come up with the production/procurement plan. The production planning module tracks the production of semi-finished and finished materials and makes them ready for the next level of consumption or shipment. In doing so, the SAP system uses materials supplied by materials management and uses internal labor and machine hours as well as overheads to produce the materials in calculating numbers for reports. Here too, a financial transaction is recorded when goods are moved into/within/outside the production department. Alex could relate to the shop-floor execution cycle at FLW.

Sales and Distribution (SD)

The *sales and distribution* module tracks activity from the start of a customer inquiry, converts it into a sales order, which is later followed-up by a shipment, and finally a sales invoice is generated. The cycle ends when the customer makes a payment (FLW called it the order-to-cash cycle). Alex did not expect a financial transaction to be generated during the inquiry and sales order stages, but he could quickly relate to the shipment, billing, and payment steps and the transactions carried out at each stage.

Finance (FI) and Controlling (CO)

Now that Alex had a good understanding of supply chain functionality and how it mapped to the MM, PP, and SD modules, Alex understood how these transactions were recorded in the financials module. Each time a goods movement or a transaction impacting finance takes place, the SAP software immediately records the financial transaction. The transaction is then typically entered in the general ledger (GL), along with accounts receivables (AR) and accounts payables (AP). Each of the transactions record profit center information and provides further detail for reporting.

It all made logical sense to Alex, but he was not able to understand what role the SAP Controlling module played in the structure. The finance training manual went on to say that SAP Controlling was all about recording transactions internally within the organization. It dealt with cost element accounting (CEA), cost center accounting (CCA), overhead cost management (OCM), activity based costing (ABC), product costing (PC), and profitability analysis (PA) — all of which support internal reporting requirements. Additionally, project systems (PS) allows tracking of a capital project and its eventual conversion to a fixed asset in the asset accounting (AA) module. Both FI and CO are integral parts of the record-to-report or accounting-to-report cycles. FLW called this process finance-to-report. A different name, but the same concept.

2.2   The link with FI

"FI is all about data capture and external reporting, whereas CO is all about internal reporting" — was highlighted in big, bold font. Alex could relate to his prior experience when it came to legal entity reporting and submitting reports to external agencies. He had to prepare a trial balance, balance sheet, and income statement, along with various other reports like cash flow statements, accounting policy, and other statutory statements per his previous employer's requirement and the law of the land.

Non-financial information, such as production volume, is not recorded in trial balance. Yet, it can be an important statistic that may be required for reporting performance to management. This would mean that there should be something that records information over and above what is required for external (legal) reporting. Is this called controlling?

The difference between FI and CO

 Financial accounting (FI) is all about data capture and external reporting, whereas controlling (CO) is all about internal reporting. FI and CO complement each other to a great extent. SAP software is an integrated system and all financial transactions are captured in financial accounting. Controlling supports internal reporting requirements.

Then why not have one single module and call it financials or reporting, or something? Alex thought. He continued reading. This is an integrated system and all transactions are captured in financial accounting. Controlling supports internal reporting requirements.

If Alex wanted to perform some sort of an allocation of costs for sending costs from one cost center to another FI could handle it. However, it would be too cumbersome to enter that type of allocation every time the source transaction occurs. CGI's software was programmed to perform the allocations at month end.

Okay, Alex thought, CGI must use controlling as part of month-end close purposes.

Month-end close has many tasks in addition to cost allocation. For example, depreciation calculation occurs in asset accounting (AA), foreign currency valuation, and accrual postings in the GL. Bank reconciliation also takes place in the banking and treasury (TR) modules, etc. — all of these tasks are handled in FI. CO passes along the work-in-progress (WIP) number to FI via the product costing module, and allows the capture of certain costs in further detail. For example, depreciation cost, which can be captured at the cost center level, allows a breakdown of where the costs are incurred. FI can be compared to a big river that brings data in from all of the tributaries (modules) and then allows for internal reporting via CO and external reporting via FI.

Alex wrote in his notes, "FI and CO complement each other to a great extent, but they may not be able to survive on their own because they are dependent on each other." He thought he now understood the crux of the link between the two modules. He was eager to know and learn more about FI and CO.

2.3   Links with other SAP modules

The finance training manual covered additional interesting links between various modules and controlling. There are links between the PP, SD, and the MM modules, but Alex was most interested in the links between supply chain functionality and the FI and CO modules, since that was going to be his job focus.

2.3.1   MM and CO-PC

Standard costs of procured materials are calculated at the beginning of the period in controlling-product costing (CO-PC). The standard cost is then used to valuate inventory, as well as record goods movements during the month in materials management (MM)

2.3.2   MM and FI-GL + FI-AP + CO-PC

Actual price on the purchase order (from MM) and on the invoice receipt from the vendor (from (FI-AP) tracks purchase price variance in accounting (in FI-GL) compared to the standard price of the material (part of CO-PC).

2.3.3   PP and CO-PC

Raw material cost is derived using quantities from the bill of material (BOM) multiplied by the raw material procurement price. Conversion cost is derived using activity quantity from routing multiplied by the predetermined activity rate. BOM and routing/recipe (recipe contains the steps to manufacture a product) are part of production planning (PP) module. Production and process orders record costs during the lifecycle of the orders and allow for WIP/variance calculations at month end.

2.3.4   PP and CO-ABC

Production/process orders use activity types that are confirmed during production to record labor and machine hours. They use predetermined activity rates through activity based costing (CO-ABC)

2.3.5   MM and FI + CO-PC

Supply purchases are directly expensed to a cost center. Raw materials are inventoried to the balance sheet. Consumption of raw materials is recorded on orders.

2.3.6   MM and FI-AA

Capital equipment purchases are recorded to an asset or capital project (part of FI-AA).

2.3.7   SD and FI-GL + FI-AR + CO-PA

Customer sales are recorded in the FI-GL and FI-AR at the time of billing to the customer. Additionally, profitability analysis (CO-PA) captures this information in multidimensional reporting known as characteristics and value fields.

2.3.8   SD and CO-CCA/CO-OM

Samples shipped to customers can be charged to a specific cost center (cost center accounting – CO-CCA) or internal orders (overhead management CO-OM) for future tracking and reporting purposes.

The training manual went on to say that **the MRP controller and financial controller are the two most powerful functions in an SAP environment.** The MRP controller decides what to produce and when to produce it, whereas the financial controller keeps track of all of the costs and variances in the plant. However, all of this depends on the demand. It is assumed that there is a constant demand for the product.

Role of MRP controller and financial controller

 MRP Controller and Financial Controller are often regarded as two key roles in an organization that uses SAP business software.

Alex remembered reading about how a manufacturing facility needs to ensure that it produces a good quality product at optimal inventory levels, while keeping a close eye on the costs. He realized that CO would help him achieve the task in his role at CGI as long as he used the available tools effectively and the processes were adhered to.

3 Controlling organization structure: It's all in the family

> *"I cannot trust a man to control others who cannot control himself."*
> — Robert E. Lee

Every organization has various departments or functions that are responsible for implementing strategic plans, converting them into action, and managing day-to-day operations. This type of functional or departmental structure is depicted in the business system as well. This chapter provides an overview of controlling organization structure in SAP business software.

Alex continued to read through the finance training manual and came across a chapter on organization structure. There was a diagram depicting overall organization structure at GCI (see Figure 3.1).

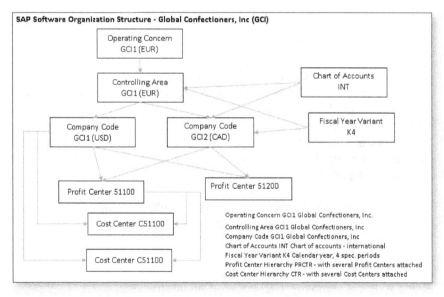

Figure 3.1: GCI SAP software organization structure

The training manual went on to further explain the importance of the SAP software organization structure.

The *SAP software organization structure* is fundamental to the overall structure in which master data and transaction data is defined in SAP. It is essentially the backbone of the system. Accurate design and setup of the software organization structure is a critical step in SAP implementation, given that it is extremely difficult to change the structure once designed, configured, and transaction data is posted.

SAP software organization structure reflects a business's own organization structure, reporting requirements, and processes in the SAP system

An enterprise's organization structure is mapped to the SAP system organization structure. This is done early on in SAP implementation projects. The idea is to ensure that all business processes are able to function smoothly, not only from a transactional processing point of view, but also from an internal and external reporting point of view.

Company code is defined based on legal entities. Since GCI has more than one legal entity, multiple company codes (for example, GCI1, GCI2, etc.) have been defined to facilitate external reporting. However, there is only one controlling area, which will allow consolidation for internal reporting.

3.1 Chart of accounts

The *chart of accounts* is a list of general ledger accounts. Accounts are broadly classified into assets and liabilities, and then in more granular detail as required by the organization. SAP is an integrated system and all transactions are recorded in the financials with GL accounts enabling data capture. The chart of accounts provides a structure for recording the transactions to enable an accurate depiction of the overall financial and operational health of the organization.

The chart of accounts can be used across multiple company codes and provides a common definition across all companies. Additionally, it streamlines the financial consolidation of the company's financial books across multiple legal entities.

Being a global company, GCI adopted an international chart of accounts (INT) that would allow capture of assets, liabilities, income, and expenses as per the international accounting standards.

Chart of accounts is maintained with configuration transaction OB13 (see Figure 3.2). The menu path is as follows: TOOLS • CUSTOMIZING • IMG • SPRO EXECUTE PROJECT • FINANCIAL ACCOUNTING (NEW) • GENERAL LEDGER ACCOUNTING (NEW) • MASTER DATA • GL ACCOUNTS • PREPARATIONS • EDIT CHART OF ACCOUNTS LIST.

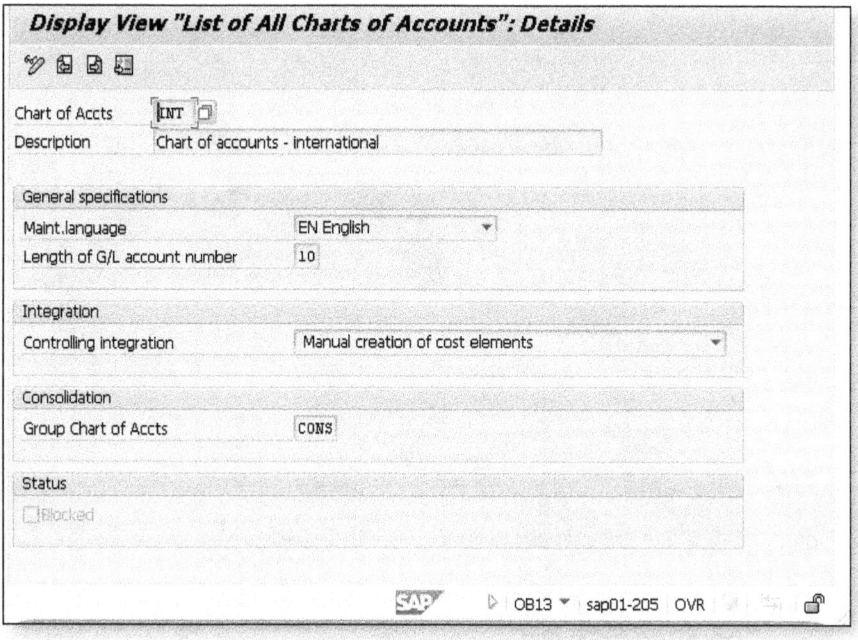

Figure 3.2: OB13— Chart of accounts

3.2   Fiscal year variant

Fiscal year variant identifies the financial and reporting calendar for an organization. GCI, like most companies, uses a calendar month as the reporting calendar and adopted fiscal year variant K4. Four periods allow for optional additional buckets for quarterly/annual financial reporting. Fiscal year variant configuration is maintained with transaction OB29 (see Figure 3.3).

The menu path is as follows: TOOLS • CUSTOMIZING • IMG • SPRO EXECUTE PROJECT • FINANCIAL ACCOUNTING (NEW) • FINANCIAL ACCOUNTING GLOBAL SETTINGS (NEW) • LEDGERS • FISCAL YEAR AND POSTING PERIODS • MAINTAIN FISCAL YEAR VARIANT.

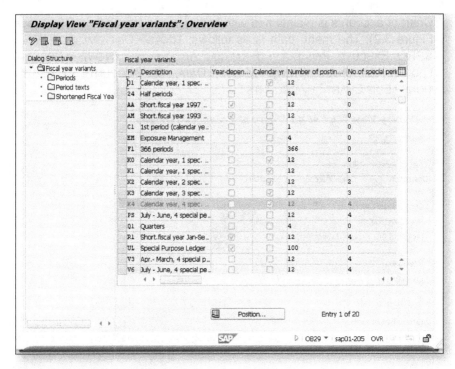

Figure 3.3: OB29 — Fiscal year variant

3.3 Operating concern

The *operating concern* depicts an enterprise from the profitability analysis point of view. It is the highest organization structure element in SAP Controlling

It is possible to assign multiple controlling areas to one operating concern. However, GCI used one controlling area, assigned to single operating concern. Operating concern is maintained with configuration transaction KEA0 (see Figure 3.4).

SAP menu path: TOOLS • CUSTOMIZING • IMG • SPRO EXECUTE PROJECT • CONTROLLING • PROFITABILITY ANALYSIS • STRUCTURES • DEFINE OPERATING CONCERN • MAINTAIN OPERATING CONCERN.

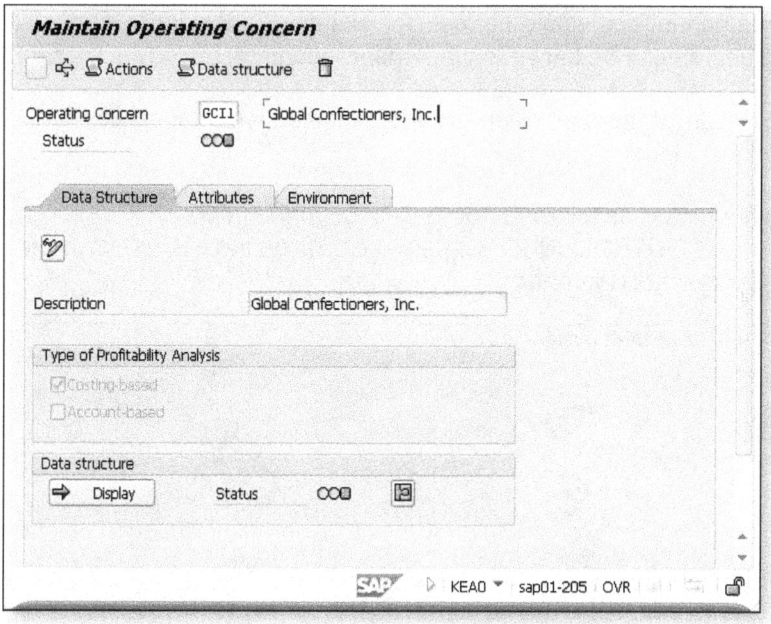

Figure 3.4: KEA0—Operating concern/Controlling area

3.4 Controlling Area

The *controlling area* captures and records costs and revenue across the organization, primarily from an internal reporting point of view. It also provides a cross-company view of the organization.

The controlling area would allow for the allocation of costs between cost centers within one controlling area.

In order to be assigned to the same controlling area, all relevant company codes must have the same chart of accounts and fiscal year variant. Although company code currency can be different, the controlling area will have a unique currency in which all transactions are recorded.

It would be possible to create multiple controlling areas, but it would not be possible to allocate costs across multiple controlling areas in a systematic way. One could, of course, post journal entries with different company codes which in turn, would post to the respective controlling areas. However, this type of allocation would not be possible using allocations in the controlling module. Additionally, consolidated management reporting capabilities would be lost (for example, operating expense reporting and other P&L based management reporting).

Configuration of the controlling area is executed with transaction OKKP as shown in Figure 3.5.

The menu path is as follows TOOLS • CUSTOMIZING • IMG • SPRO EXECUTE PROJECT • CONTROLLING • GENERAL CONTROLLING • ORGANIZATION • MAINTAIN CONTROLLING AREA.

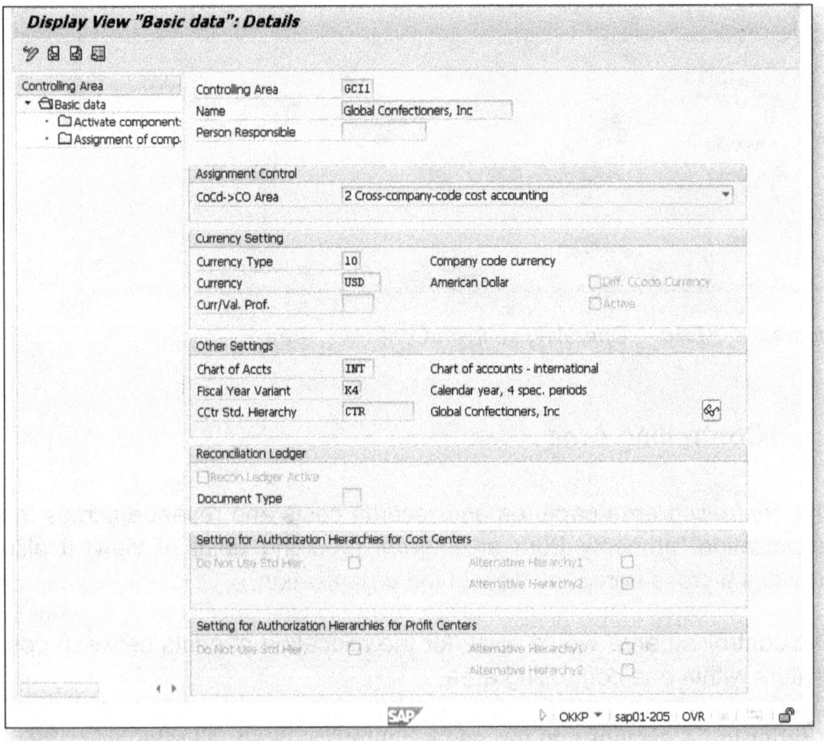

Figure 3.5: OKKP — Controlling area

3.5   Company Code

Company code is the smallest organizational unit for which a complete set of self-contained accounts can be drawn up for external reporting.

A company code represents a legal entity for external reporting and records all relevant transactions and generates all supporting documents for the legally required financial statements, such as balance sheet and P&L. Company code is setup using configuration transaction OX02 and maintained using configuration transaction OBY6 as shown in Figure 3.6.

SAP menu path for company code setup: TOOLS • CUSTOMIZING • IMG • SPRO EXECUTE PROJECT • ENTERPRISE STRUCTURE • DEFINITION • FINANCIAL ACCOUNTING • EDIT, COPY, DELETE, CHECK COMPANY CODE

SAP menu path for company code global parameters: TOOLS • CUSTOMIZING • IMG • SPRO EXECUTE PROJECT • FINANCIAL ACCOUNTING (NEW) • FINANCIAL ACCOUNTING GLOBAL SETTINGS (NEW) • GLOBAL PARAMETERS FOR COMPANY CODE • ENTER GLOBAL PARAMETERS.

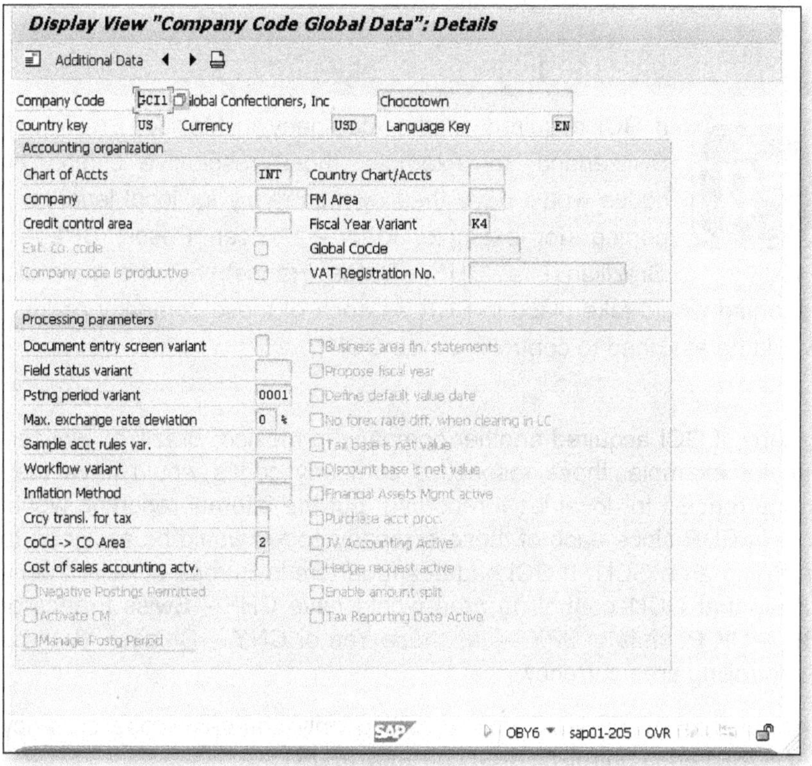

Figure 3.6: OBY6 — Company code

It is possible to post cross-company transactions within financial accounting (FI), provided affiliates are set up as customers and vendors, defined as trading partners. One can perform intercompany eliminations based on trading partner information.

3.5.1 Currencies

GCI assigned both company codes GCI1 (Currency USD — US Dollars) and GCI2 (Currency CAD — Canadian Dollars) to controlling area GCI1 (Currency EUR — Euro). Additionally, GCI set up *additional local currencies for company code* in configuration transaction OB22 (see Figure 3.7).

The menu path is as follows: TOOLS • CUSTOMIZING • IMG • SPRO EXECUTE PROJECT • FINANCIAL ACCOUNTING GLOBAL SETTINGS • COMPANY CODE • PARALLEL CURRENCIES • DEFINE ADDITIONAL LOCAL CURRENCIES.

This effectively means that company code GCI1 records transactions in both currencies (USD and EUR). Company code GCI2 records transactions in two currencies — CAD and EUR

Currencies in controlling area and company code

 If GCI acquired another company in Mexico, Brazil, or Switzerland, for example, those respective company codes would have their own currency for local legal reporting (for example, MXN — Mexican Pesos, BRL — Brazilian Lira, CHF — Swiss Francs), but the internal reporting would take place in EUR as each of these company codes would be assigned to controlling area GCI1.

Similarly, if GCI acquired another company in Mexico, Brazil, or Switzerland, for example, those respective company codes would have their own currencies for local legal reporting, but the internal reporting would occur in EUR since each of these company codes would be assigned to controlling area GCI1. If GCI had headquarters in Europe or Asia, then it is likely that GCI1 controlling area would have CHF — Swiss Francs or GBP — UK Pounds or JPY — Japanese Yen or CNY — Chinese Yuan as its controlling area currency.

The company is not limited to recording only company code currency (CAD/USD) and controlling area currency (EUR).

Financial accounting captures transaction currency (for example, SGD — Singapore Dollars) at the financial accounting document level (also known as document currency). This transaction in SGD is translated at the prevailing exchange rate into company code currency (also known as first local currency). Additionally, controlling area currency is also recorded as second local currency (also known as group currency). Thus, financial accounting records three currencies — transaction / document currency, company code/local currency and controlling area/group currency.

Currencies in financial accounting (FI) and controlling (CO)

Financial accounting records transactions in: transaction/document currency, company code/local currency, and controlling area/group currency.

Controlling records transactions in: transaction/document currency, object currency (same as company code currency), and controlling area currency.

Alex noted that the names of these fields were a bit different between FI and CO, but that they essentially stored the same values in both modules.

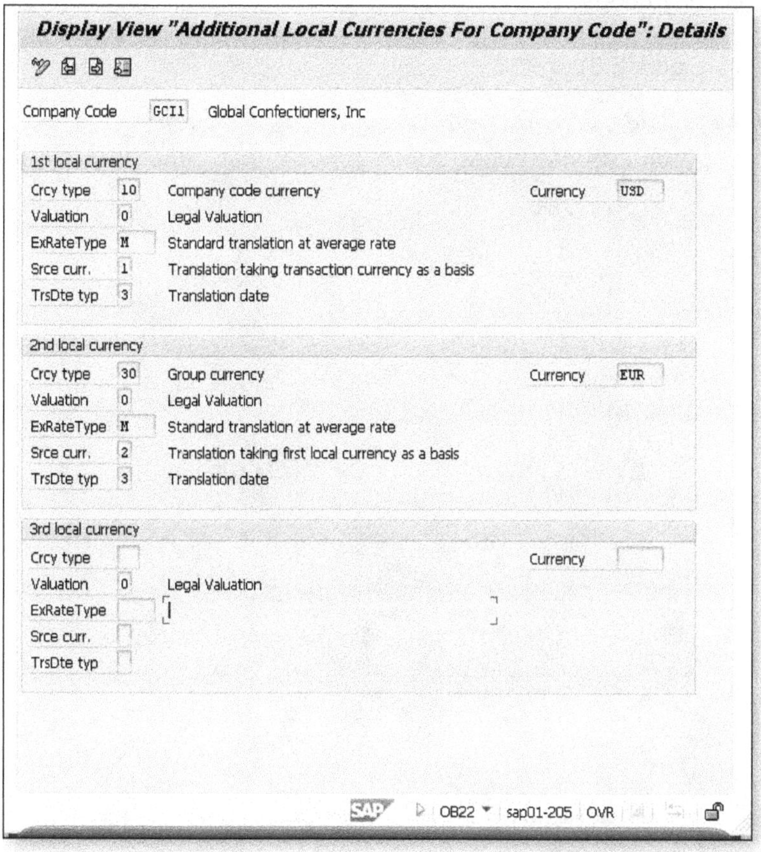

Display View "Additional Local Currencies For Company Code": Details

Company Code GCI1 Global Confectioners, Inc

1st local currency

Crcy type	10	Company code currency	Currency	USD
Valuation	0	Legal Valuation		
ExRateType	M	Standard translation at average rate		
Srce curr.	1	Translation taking transaction currency as a basis		
TrsDte typ	3	Translation date		

2nd local currency

Crcy type	30	Group currency	Currency	EUR
Valuation	0	Legal Valuation		
ExRateType	M	Standard translation at average rate		
Srce curr.	2	Translation taking first local currency as a basis		
TrsDte typ	3	Translation date		

3rd local currency

Crcy type			Currency	
Valuation	0	Legal Valuation		
ExRateType				
Srce curr.				
TrsDte typ				

SAP ▷ OB22 ▼ sap01-205 OVR

Figure 3.7: OB22 — Additional local currencies for company code

33

3.6 Profit center

A *profit center* is a business unit in the enterprise that can act as an independent unit operating in the marketplace. One can monitor both income and expenses at the profit center level and thus, create a complete P&L (and even a partial balance sheet at the working capital level) at the profit center level. This information can then be summarized using the profit center hierarchy to depict the management structure. Alternative hierarchy structures can also be defined for summarized analysis, for example, by sector or business/location to report and manage operating results.

Objects such as cost centers, projects, materials, sales orders, etc. are assigned to a profit center. This allows costs and revenues to flow at profit center level for reporting. A profit center can be assigned to one or many company codes for a cross-company code view for internal management reporting. Profit center hierarchy is set up using transaction KCH1 (see Figure 3.8).

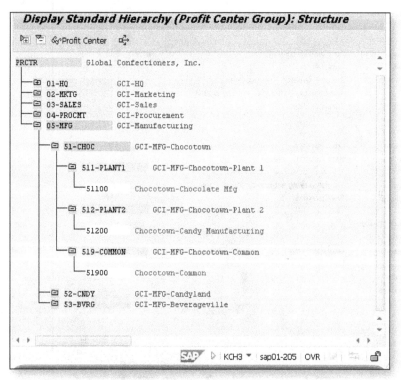

Figure 3.8: KCH1 — Profit center hierarchy

The menu path is as follows: ACCOUNTING • CONTROLLING • PROFIT CENTER ACCOUNTING • MASTER DATA • STANDARD HIERARCHY • CREATE.

3.7 Controlling versions

Versions in SAP Controlling maintain independent sets of planning data and actual data.

Versions are used in planning to set up alternative scenarios based on different assumptions. Different versions can represent best case, worst case, or most likely scenarios. Other examples are different markets, promotional campaigns, and sales strategies.

The most likely scenario is usually set up in plan version 000. This data is used to calculate planned prices for activity types. Actual data is posted in version 000 to compare plan versus actual, as well as plan versus target.

Use transaction OKEQ to configure controlling versions as shown in Figure 3.9.

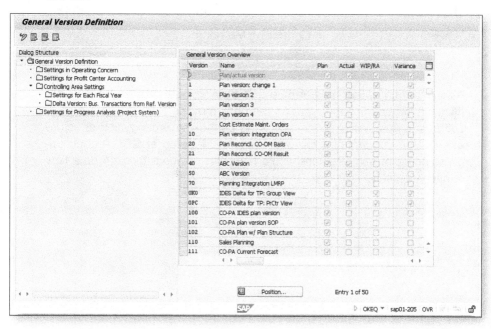

Figure 3.9: OKEQ — Controlling versions

The menu path is as follows: TOOLS • CUSTOMIZING • IMG • SPRO EXE-CUTE PROJECT • ENTERPRISE STRUCTURE • CONTROLLING • GENERAL CONTROLLING • ORGANIZATION • MAINTAIN VERSIONS

3.8 Summary

Alex prepared a list of transactions to set up CGI's controlling organization structure (see Table 3.1).

Transaction Code	Description
OB13	Chart of Accounts
OB29	Fiscal Year Variant
KEA0	Operating Concern
OKKP	Controlling Area
OBY6	Company Code
OB22	Additional Local Currencies
KCH3	Profit Center Hierarchy / Group
OKEQ	Controlling Versions

Table 3.1: Transactions to set up controlling organization structure

Alex understood that master data and transactional data in the SAP application is heavily dependent on the design of the SAP software organization structure. After he reviewed the controlling organization structure at GCI, Alex understood the overall technical setup at GCI. A good understanding of this structure would help him navigate through data flow relatively quickly.

4 Controlling master data: So simple, yet so complex (keep it straight, or else...)

"Whenever you are asked if you can do a job, tell 'em, 'Certainly I can!' Then get busy and find out how to do it."
— Theodore Roosevelt

Master data plays a very critical role in ensuring the effectiveness of a system. It sounds simple, but meeting competing requirements of various functions (or at times even under various business processes within the same function) can be challenging. Consistency and accuracy of master data maintenance contributes significantly towards realizing business benefits from a system. We will review controlling master data elements in this chapter.

"As you know," Bob said to Alex one morning, "we are setting up a new production line in our plant. We need to create cost centers and all of the related system setup to get this line up and running. Can you go through the system manual and find all of the steps required to complete this task? You may want to reach out to Erin, she is very knowledgeable and can help you if you have any questions."

"Sure, I will work on it, Bob," said Alex. Alex turned his attention to the training guide. He had finished the sections regarding the SAP controlling organization structure at GCI1, he now went on to read about SAP controlling master data.

From his prior experience at Fork-of-Lift Works (FLW), Alex was aware that master data plays an important role in any system, regardless of whether it is an integrated ERP application such as SAP, or a home-grown system that may or may not be well integrated.

If we were to visualize organization structure, master data, and transaction data in a pyramid form, organization structure sits at the top of the pyramid, the master data layer is at the center of the pyramid, and the transaction processing layer is at the bottom of the pyramid. Master data inherits a lot of organization structure information and passes it along to the transaction processing layer. Hence, it is important to define organization structure, as well as master data attributes during the design phase and build on the design on an ongoing basis.

Once defined, it is not necessary to make frequent changes in the organization structure. However, the master data needs to be maintained on an ongoing basis.

Additionally, master data maintenance is handled by the business — typically directly in the production environment. Accurate maintenance of master data is important to ensure consistent capture of data on the transaction processing layer.

4.1 Cost centers — Where did we spend all of the money?

A *cost center* is one of the most widely used master data elements in controlling. Cost centers allow departmental breakdown of costs. They are often the lowest level of an organization where one wants to collect and analyze costs and departmental performance. Cost centers are therefore useful for the purpose of departmental budgets and plan versus actual comparison of expenses. Cost centers can also be used for the purpose of interdepartmental cost allocations through sender-receiver relationships. The relationships can be defined in cost center allocations — some of the widely used methods are distribution and assessments.

Cost centers are structured into organizational and/or functional hierarchical groups. Each cost center is assigned to a cost center hierarchy and a profit center.

Cost center definition, examples

 A cost center is an organizational unit in a controlling area that represents a defined location of cost incurrence. A cost center can be created based on functional requirements (a department or section), allocation criteria (maintenance costs that are allocated to a pool to manufacturing cost centers), physical location (headquarters, manufacturing facility 1, manufacturing facility 2, distribution center 1, and distribution center 2), and responsibility for costs (finance, accounting, legal, and marketing).

Usually cost centers are setup for a function, machine, responsibility center, or a physical location that is permanent, or at least long-term in nature. For example, if you need to set up the new production line that Bob was referring to, cost center is the correct controlling object. However, if you need to track costs for a short-term productivity improvement project or a targeted marketing campaign that is temporary in nature, then an *internal order* is a better option than a cost center.

4.1.1 Cost center hierarchy

Cost center hierarchy consists of groups of cost centers in a tree structure within a controlling area.

Cost centers can be grouped together to provide summary cost information. A cost center hierarchy consists of nodes and sub-nodes that cost centers are attached to.

A cost center hierarchy comprises all cost centers for a given period and therefore, represents the entire enterprise. This hierarchy is known as the *standard hierarchy*.

Cost center hierarchies are typically defined before creating cost centers. Maintenance is handled via transaction OKENN (see Figure 4.1).

The menu path is as follows: ACCOUNTING • CONTROLLING • COST CENTER ACCOUNTING • MASTER DATA • STANDARD HIERARCHY • CHANGE (OKEON) / DISPLAY (OKENN).

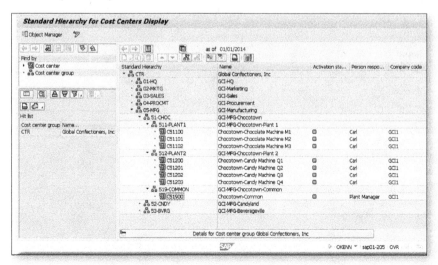

Figure 4.1: OKENN—Cost center standard hierarchy

4.1.2 Cost center maintenance

Cost centers are organizational units in a controlling area that represent a defined location of a cost incurrence. The definition can be based on functional requirements, allocation criteria, physical location, or responsibility for costs.

The cost center defines the smallest area of responsibility within the company that causes and influences costs, meaning the lowest level to which you can meaningfully assign *direct costs* and *indirect costs*.

Cost centers are assigned to a single company code (legal entity), a single profit center (performance entity), a single functional area (type of function), and a single cost center category (what kind of costs can be planned or booked to).

Cost centers are used to plan, capture, track, and report departmental expenses and services consumed or provided by a department using cost center accounting.

Cost centers are maintained via transaction KS01 (Create), KS02 (Change) (see Figure 4.2), KS03 (Display), and KS04 (Delete).

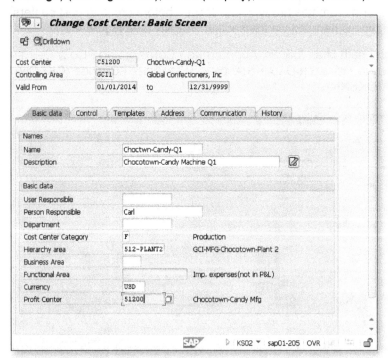

Figure 4.2: KS02 — Cost center change

The menu path is as follows: ACCOUNTING • CONTROLLING • COST CENTER ACCOUNTING • MASTER DATA • COST CENTER • INDIVIDUAL PROCESSING • CREATE (KS01) / CHANGE (KS02) / DISPLAY (KS03) / DELETE (KS04).

Mass maintenance of cost centers can be carried out using transaction KS12 (see Figure 4.3).

The menu path is as follows: ACCOUNTING • CONTROLLING • COST CENTER ACCOUNTING • MASTER DATA • COST CENTER • COLLECTIVE PROCESSING • CHANGE (KS12) / DISPLAY (KS13) / DELETE (KS14).

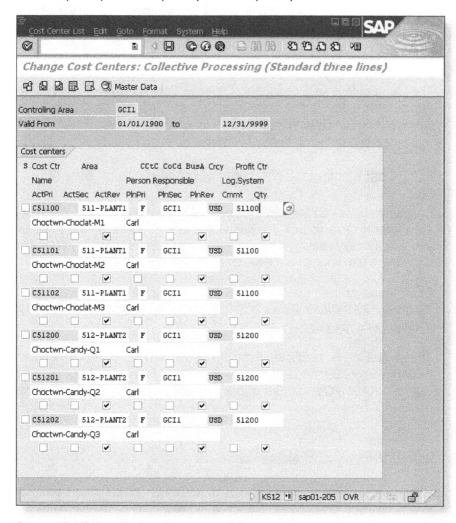

Figure 4.3: KS12 — Cost center mass maintenance

4.1.3 Cost center groups

Cost center groups collect cost centers according to various criteria into groups to enable cost centers to depict the structure of the organization in the system.

Cost center groups are also referred to as *alternative hierarchies*.

Cost center groups utilize groups to build cost center hierarchies, which summarize the decision-making, responsibility and control areas according to the particular requirements of the organization. The individual cost centers form the lowest hierarchical level.

Cost center groups are maintained using transaction KSH2.

The menu path is as follows: ACCOUNTING • CONTROLLING • COST CENTER ACCOUNTING • MASTER DATA • COST CENTER GROUP • CREATE (KSH1) / CHANGE (KSH2) / DISPLAY (KSH3).

4.2 Cost elements—What kind of money is being spent?

Cost element can be defined as a vehicle for carrying costs in CO. They are similar to GL accounts. They provide a view for management on where and how money is being spent. It allows management to identify a specific area where the organization may need to focus on controlling costs.

Cost elements are maintained via transaction KA01 (Create), KA02 (Change), KA03 (see Figure 4.4) (Display), KA04 (Delete), and KA06 (Create Secondary).

The menu path is as follows: ACCOUNTING • CONTROLLING • COST CENTER ACCOUNTING • MASTER DATA • COST ELEMENT • INDIVIDUAL PROCESSING • CREATE (KA01) / CREATE SECONDARY (KA06) / CHANGE (KA02) / DISPLAY (KA03) / DELETE (KA04).

4.2.1 Primary cost elements

Primary cost elements create the link between FI and CO. In general, for every P&L type GL account in finance, corresponding cost elements are created in controlling. These elements are called primary cost elements. There may be some exceptions where not all GL accounts are created as cost elements. For example, interest expense, when management does not want to track interest expense by a cost center.

The following cost element categories are used to create primary cost elements:

▶ 01 — Primary cost element: Can be debited with all primary postings, for example, in FI or MM.

▶ 11 — Revenue element: Used to post revenues.

▶ 12 — Sales deduction: Used to post sales deductions, adjustments, or deduction postings of revenues, such as discounts and rebates.

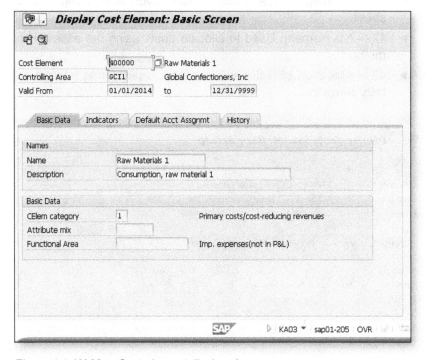

Figure 4.4: KA03 — Cost element display

4.2.2 Secondary cost elements

Secondary cost elements (see Figure 4.5) can be created to record controlling-specific transactions such as settlement, overhead rates, assessment, and activity allocation. They describe cost flows that occur within SAP Controlling. Unlike primary cost elements, there is no link to the GL account in FI.

The following cost element categories can be used for secondary cost elements:

▶ 21 — Internal settlement: Used to settle (further allocate) order or project costs to CO-internal objects. CO-internal objects are, for example, orders, profitability segments, cost centers, and projects.

▶ 31 — Order/project results analysis: System-required accounts for posting WIP.

▶ 41 — Overhead rates: Used to load overheads using costing sheet.

▶ 42 — Assessment: Used to allocate costs using the assessment method.

▶ 43 — Allocation of activities/processes: Used during internal activity allocation.

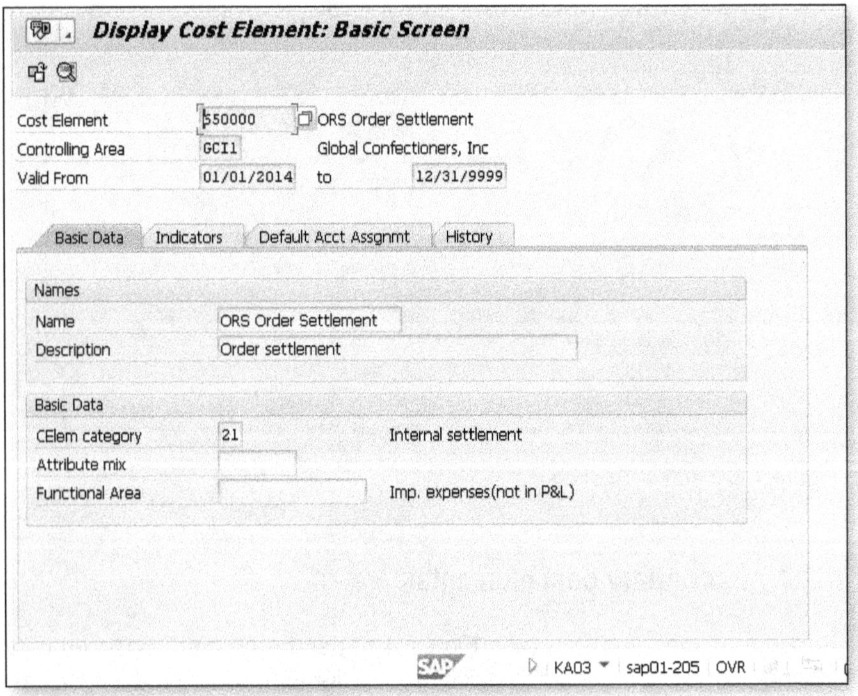

Figure 4.5: KA03 — Secondary cost element display

4.2.3 Cost element groups

Cost element groups collect cost elements with similar characteristics.

Cost element groups can be utilized for reporting, for example, using the cost element group structure to define the row structure of the reports.

Cost element groups can also be used when several cost elements need to be used in one transaction, for example, in cost center planning, distribution, or assessment.

Cost element groups use transaction KAH1 (Create), KAH2 (Change), and KAH3 (Display) (see Figure 4.6).

The menu path is as follows: ACCOUNTING • CONTROLLING • COST CENTER ACCOUNTING • MASTER DATA • COST ELEMENT GROUP • CREATE (KAH1) / CHANGE (KAH2) / DISPLAY (KAH3).

Figure 4.6: KAH3— Cost element group display

4.3 Activity types — Are these the cost drivers that we keep talking about all of the time?

Activity types classify the activities produced in the cost centers within a controlling area. The activity type represents the activities performed in a cost center, for example labor hours, or maintenance hours for a maintenance cost center.

Activity types describe the specific activity output provided by a cost center to other cost objects like work orders, internal orders, etc. They are measured in units of time and quantity, and valued using a rate per hour or per unit of activity.

- ▶ Total planned cost / Planned activity hours = Planned activity rate per hour
- ▶ Total actual cost / Actual activity hours = Actual activity rate per hour

Activity types are maintained using transaction KL01 (Create), KL02 (Change), KL03 (Display) (see Figure 4.7), KL04 (Delete)

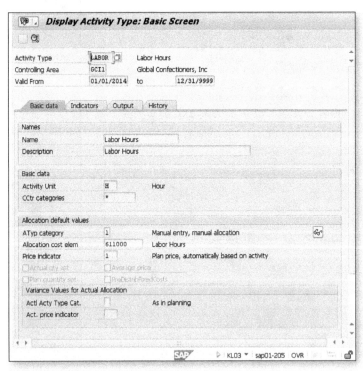

Figure 4.7: KL03 — Activity type display

46

The menu path is as follows: ACCOUNTING • CONTROLLING • COST CENTER ACCOUNTING • MASTER DATA • ACTIVITY TYPE • INDIVIDUAL PROCESSING • CREATE (KL01) / CHANGE (KL02) / DISPLAY (KL03) / DELETE (KL04).

4.4 SKFs—It is all statistical data after all

A *statistical key figure (SKF)* is used to track quantities and values for various operating activities. SKFs are designed for use in reporting and analysis and can also be used to assist in the allocation of costs.

An SKF can be defined either as a fixed value or a total value. Key figures defined as fixed values are valid as of the posting period and in all subsequent posting periods of the fiscal year. In contrast, key figures defined as total values are only valid for the posting period in which they are entered.

SKFs are maintained via transaction KK01 (Create), KK02 (Change), KK03 (Display) (see Figure 4.8), and K03DEL (Delete).

The menu path is as follows: ACCOUNTING • CONTROLLING • COST CENTER ACCOUNTING • MASTER DATA • STATISTICAL KEY FIGURES • INDIVIDUAL PRO-CESSING • CREATE (KK01) / CHANGE (KK02) / DISPLAY (KK03) / DELETE (KK03DEL).

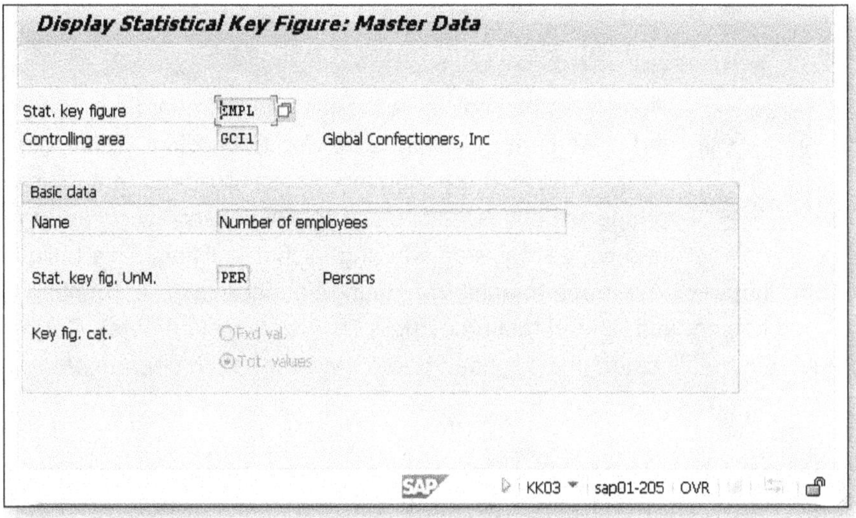

Figure 4.8: KK03 — Statistical key figure display

4.5   Allocations—who is sending, who is receiving—an internal Web?

A typical manufacturing facility incurs costs in various departments. For example, the maintenance department can provide a service to the production department to keep the machines running. Similarly, the information systems department helps keep the systems running. Usually, the goal is to transfer costs from these service departments to production departments, so that the costs get added to the cost of the product. This transfer of costs internally within controlling is achieved using *allocations*.

There are two main types of allocations in controlling: distribution and assessments.

Using *distribution*, the following information is retained and passed on to the receivers: the original, primary cost element. The sender and receiver information is documented with line items in the CO document.

Using *assessments*, the following information is passed on to the receivers: original cost elements are grouped together into assessment cost elements (secondary cost elements); original cost elements are not displayed on the receivers.

The sender and receiver information is displayed in the CO document.

Distribution versus assessment

 Here is an example of a facilities department (one sending cost center) responsible for a building. This cost center incurs three primary costs: building rent, telephone expenses, and beverage expenses (such as tea and coffee) for staff working in that building. This building houses four departments: marketing, finance and accounting, purchasing, and human resources (four receiving cost centers). Costs should be allocated in predefined percentages for each department.

If the *distribution* method of allocation is used, then the same primary cost element is used to allocate costs. The sender cost center gets a credit using three original primary cost elements. Four receiving cost centers will each see three original primary cost elements as debits to their cost centers. This means each department is able to identify how much money was allocated on each of the three expense categories of rent, telephone, and beverage.

If the *assessment* method of allocation is used, then a secondary cost element for assessment, say *facilities expense*, is used to allocate costs. The sender cost center gets a credit via the assessment cost element. Four receiving cost centers will each see one secondary cost element as a debit to their cost center. This means each department only knows how much money was allocated to them under *facilities expense*. The receivers do not know how much of this facilities expense consists of rent, telephone, and beverage. One would need to look up a report for the sending cost center to identify the breakdown of these costs.

4.6   Internal orders—yet another tool for cost tracking?

Internal orders are used to collect, monitor, and settle direct and indirect costs incurred by a specific project.

They are cost collectors that have a more dynamic nature than cost or profit centers.

Orders can be used as a primary cost object which is then settled to a cost center or as a statistical posting object where the primary posting goes to the cost center.

Plan data can be entered for orders and can be tracked against actual spend.

Internal orders can be used for a variety of purposes in CO, a few examples are provided next.

Internal order examples

 An internal order is created for a customer event to track budget and actual amounts for the event. Once the event is completed, costs are settled (or moved) to the appropriate cost center.

Vehicle repair and maintenance costs are booked to one cost center, but the costs for each vehicle are also tracked "statistically" using a statistical internal order created for each vehicle.

Each research and development (R&D) project requires tracking of actual spending. R&D internal orders help capture of individual project's costs.

4.7 Summary

Alex now turned to Bob's request to list all of the steps that were necessary to reflect the new production line in the system. Since the chart of accounts was common, Alex did not think that there was a need to set up additional cost elements. Additionally, the design required that a common set of activity types and statistical key figures (SKFs) be used. Therefore, there was no need to set up new activity types or SKFs.

Controlling master data changes necessary for a new production line include:

- ▶ KS01 — Create new cost center, under the same hierarchy node as that of existing lines ("512-PLANT2").
- ▶ KSH2 — Add new cost center in alternate cost center group for Chocotown.
- ▶ KSV8 — Create a new *segment* in plan distribution for new cost center.
- ▶ KSV2 — Create a new segment in actual distribution for new cost center.

Alex learned that consistent ongoing maintenance of master data is fundamental to the accuracy of transaction data and reporting. Given the sensitive nature of the data, GCI has centralized access to create and change data to a handful of individuals. Display access was relatively broad, as several business users may need to review this data from time to time.

Since there were many transactions referred to in the training manual, Alex made a small table as a quick reference tool (see Figure 4.9).

Controlling Master Data Objects and their transaction codes					
Controlling Master Data Object	Create	Change	Display	Delete *	Mass Change	Mass Display
Cost Center	KS01	KS02	KS03	KS04	KS12	KS13
Cost Center Group	KSH1	KSH2	KSH3			
Cost Element (Primary)	KA01	KA02	KA03	KA04		KA24
Cost Element (Secondary)	KA06	KA02	KA03	KA04		
Cost Element Group	KAH1	KAH2	KAH3			
Activity Type	KL01	KL02	KL03	KL04	KL12	KL13
Activity Type Group	KLH1	KLH2	KLH3			
Statistical Key Figure	KK01	KK02	KK03	KK03DEL	KAK2	KAK3
Statistical Key Figure Group	KBH1	KBH2	KBH3			
Internal Order	KO01	KO02	KO03		KOK2	KOK3
Internal Order Group	KOH1	KOH2	KOH3			
* Object cannot be deleted if transaction data exists for the given fiscal year						

Allocation Object **	Create	Change	Display	Execute
Plan Distribution	KSV7	KSV8	KSV9	KSVB
Plan Assessment	KSU7	KSU8	KSU9	KSUB
Actual Distribution	KSV1	KSV2	KSV3	KSV5
Actual Assessment	KSU1	KSU2	KSU3	KSU5
** Distribution / Assessment will be covered with further details in subsequent chapters				

Figure 4.9: Controlling master data objects and transaction codes

5 Planning on cost centers: An annual marathon?

> "Let our advance worrying become advance thinking and planning."
> — Winston Churchill

Most organizations undergo an annual budgeting (or planning) process that helps them prepare for the upcoming year. Various planning methods may involve a combination or use of one of the methods, like taking the previous year's plan as the base, previous twelve months actual as the base, or even planning from scratch (popularly referred to as zero based budgeting). The planning process typically starts with sales and operations (S&OP) planning, which is then broken down into production plan, procurement plan, labor cost plan, and overhead cost plan. This chapter will provide an overview of cost center planning, which typically covers overhead planning and labor cost planning.

The ultimate goal of a manufacturing unit is to consistently deliver throughput at a consistent quality, while maintaining optimum inventory levels. In doing so, it must accurately determine and control the cost at which it has produced this material.

Product costs include direct costs, as well as indirect costs. Direct costs are comprised of the cost of raw materials, packaging materials, and all the direct conversion costs of producing the finished material. This would typically include the costs of those personnel who have 'touched' the product (those directly involved in manufacturing the product). Indirect costs include the cost of those personnel who may not have directly "touched" the product, but have indirectly contributed in producing the material. For example, maintenance staff, housekeeping staff, warehouse staff, security, finance, human resources, facilities, systems, etc.

Another way to look at the conversion cost is that a product must *carry* (or absorb) the cost of the departments it passes through. Predetermined absorption rate is used to load the product with the cost of department.

For example, if the total planned budget for a department is $10,000.00 for the month with 200 hours of planned operation, the predetermined absorption rate is $10,000.00 / 200 hours = $ 50.00/hr.

This cost can be further broken down into labor hours, machine hours, and any other additional cost drivers based on the business requirement. These drivers are often defined as an *activity type* in the SAP system.

At GCI, labor hours and machine hours are defined as the two main activity types. These drivers have a rate called an *activity rate*, or *planned activity rate.*

Alex remembered FLW used similar cost drivers in their legacy system—direct labor hours, indirect labor hours, and machine hours. However, at FLW they were called *burden rate.*

GCI carried out their planning cycle during August through November. The sales team created the sales forecast at SKU level for the upcoming year. The production planning team compared the demand to the capacity and arrived at the planned production volume. The planning team could then arrive at the planned procurement of raw materials. Alex recalled the methodology at FLW—planning was not as detailed and was often done at the product group level. However, he could relate to the objective of the exercise, as manufacturing must always be operationally ready for the next year!

Planned exchange rates for various currency combinations need to be maintained for the planning period before feeding plan data into the system for the next year. This ensures that all plan costs are converted at a consistent exchange rate.

Alex decided to learn the system using a hands-on example. He logged into a test system and started entering plan data step by step, following the instructions in the user manual.

5.1 Activity quantity planning

Step 1: Set planner profile (KP04)

The first step in cost center planning is to set the *planner profile* using transaction KP04. Use the planner profile to pick and choose the right combination of fields suitable for your planning needs. GCI decided to use the SAP-delivered standard planner profile SAPALL (see Figure 5.1), which includes all possible combinations for planning.

The menu path is as follows: ACCOUNTING • CONTROLLING • COST CENTER ACCOUNTING • PLANNING • SET PLANNER PROFILE.

Figure 5.1: KP04 — Set planner profile

Step 2: Activity quantity planning (KP26) — cost centers

The next step in cost center planning is to carry out *activity quantity planning* to determine the base for absorption. Typically, the activity quantity will be determined by the production volume for the planning period, which can be further constrained by production capacity and potential downtime for maintenance, if any.

As shown in Figure 5.2, the initial KP26 screen requires you to enter the version, periods, and year that you are conducting planning for. Additionally, enter the cost center (or cost center group) and activity type (or activity type group). Last, select entries in free form (where the user enters the values) or form-based (where the system pre-populates possible combinations of master data and the user enters the quantities). GCI decided to use free form for entering plan data.

The menu path is as follows: ACCOUNTING • CONTROLLING • COST CENTER ACCOUNTING • PLANNING • ACTIVITY OUTPUT/PRICES • CHANGE.

In this example, Alex wanted to see what planning for cost center group 51-CHOC would look like for 2014.

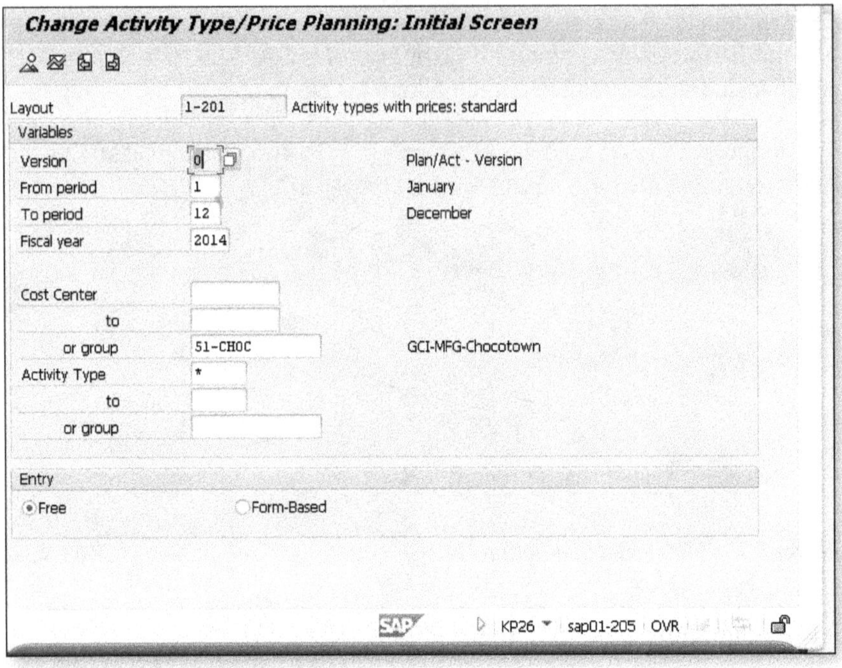

Figure 5.2: KP26 — Initial activity quantity planning screen

Once Alex clicked on the OVERVIEW icon on the initial screen, the overview screen appeared (see Figure 5.3). Two activities were planned — labor for 6,000 hours for the year and MCHRS (machine hours) for 1,800 hours for the year.

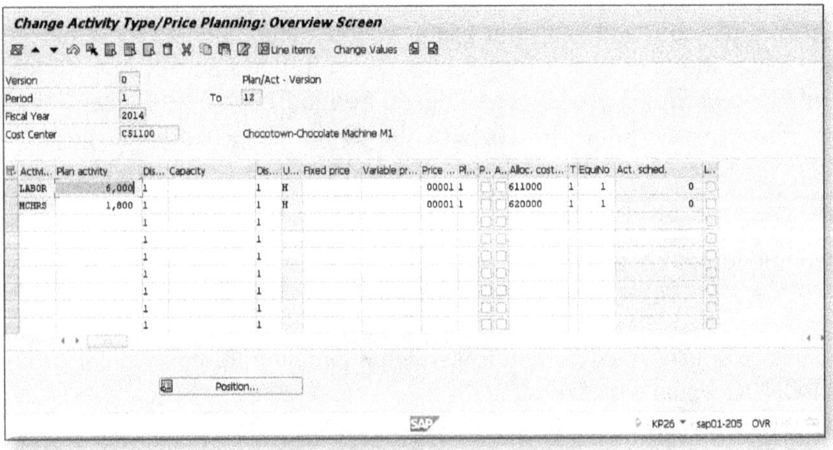

Figure 5.3: KP26 — Activity quantity planning overview screen

When Alex clicked on the Period screen (see Figure 5.4), he saw that the 6,000 hours planned for labor were distributed evenly across 12 months. Alex could plan for different activity quantities for each month, as would usually be the case in manufacturing setup, however, for the purpose of this example, Alex decided to use evenly distributed activity quantities.

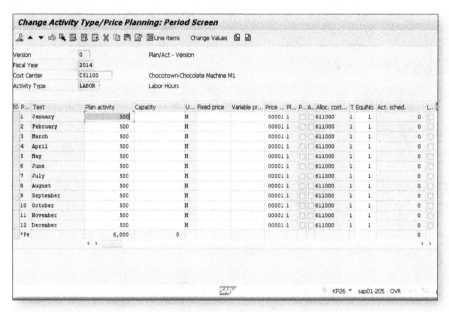

Figure 5.4: KP26 — Activity quantity planning period screen

5.2 Direct costs (activity dependent)

Step 3: Activity dependent cost planning (KP06)

Now that the quantities were planned, it was time to plan for the dollars (or amounts).

The KP06 screen (see Figure 5.5) looked very similar to KP26 –except that there was an additional field for the cost element.

The menu path is as follows: Accounting • Controlling • Cost Center Accounting • Planning • Cost and Activity Inputs • Change.

Additionally, the same screen is used for both *activity dependent cost planning*, as well as *activity independent cost planning*. If you leave the ACTIVITY TYPE field blank, then it would result in activity *independent* cost planning. However, if the activity type field was populated with a "*" or a specific activity, then it would result in activity *dependent* cost planning. Fixed cost planning is usually activity independent in nature, given that these costs would occur regardless of whether any tasks were performed.

Planning for activity dependent/independent costs

 Activity independent cost planning is carried out by leaving the ACTIVITY TYPE field blank on KP06 initial screen. Activity dependent cost planning is carried out by entering a "*" or a specific ACTIVITY TYPE on the initial screen.

Change Cost Element/Activity Input Planning: Initial Screen

Layout	1-101	Cost elements acty-indep./acty-dependent
Variables		
Version	0	Plan/Act - Version
From period	1	January
To period	12	December
Fiscal year	2014	
Cost Center		
to		
or group	51-CHOC	GCI-MFG-Chocotown
Activity Type	*	
to		
or group		
Cost Element	*	
to		
or group		

Entry

● Free   ○ Form-Based

Figure 5.5: KP06 — Initial activity dependent cost planning screen

As shown in Figure 5.6, Alex went ahead and planned for activity LABOR with cost elements 420000 (direct labor costs) and 449000 (other personnel costs). He ensured that the dollars planned for this combination were entered in the PLAN VARIABLE COSTS column due to the nature of these costs — variable costs directly proportional to activity quantity.

Next, Alex planned for activity MCHRS using cost elements 452000 (machine maintenance) and 481000 (Cost accounting depreciation) — both fixed in nature — and 416200 (electricity use) which is variable in nature.

Change Cost Element/Activity Input Planning: Overview Screen

Version	0	Plan/Act - Version
Period	1	To 12
Fiscal Year	2014	
Cost Center	C51100	Chocotown-Chocolate Machine M1

Activi...	Cost elem...	Plan fixed costs	Dis...	Plan variable costs	Dis...	Plan fixed consu...	Dis...	Plan vbl consum...	Dis...	U...	Q	L..
LABOR	420000		1	120,000.00	1	0.000	1	0.000	1			
	449000		1	60,000.00	1	0.000	1	0.000	1			
MCHRS	416200		1	18,000.00	1	0.000	1	0.000	1			
	452000	36,000.00	1		1	0.000	1	0.000	1			
	481000	72,000.00	1		1	0.000	1	0.000	1			
*Activ	*Cost elem	108,000.00		198,000.00		0.000		0.000				
			1		1		1		1			
			1		1		1		1			
			1		1		1		1			
			1		1		1		1			
			1		1		1		1			
			1		1		1		1			

Position...

KP06 ▾ sap01-205 OVR

Figure 5.6: KP06 — Activity dependent cost planning overview screen

After entering plan data for activity dependent costs, Alex wanted to see what the report would look like. He navigated to transaction code S_ALR_87013611 (see Figure 5.7), which provided the actual/plan/variance data for cost centers. Since there was no actual data in the test system, all Alex could see was the planning data he entered.

The menu path is as follows: ACCOUNTING • CONTROLLING • COST CENTER ACCOUNTING • INFORMATION SYSTEM • PLAN/ACTUAL COMPARISONS • COST CENTERS: ACTUAL/PLAN/VARIANCE.

Alex noticed there was data on the debit side, but the credit side was blank. The credit side information will be populated once plan price calculation (transaction KSPI) is carried out.

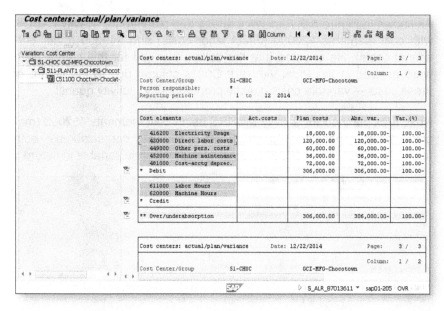

Figure 5.7: S_ALR_87013611 — Cost centers: actual /plan/ variance report (after activity dependent planning is carried out)

5.3 Overhead costs (activity independent)

Step 4: Activity independent cost planning (KP06)

Alex now moved on to enter fixed cost information in transaction KP06 (see Figure 5.8), which is independent of the activity being performed in the department. This would require that he needs to leave the ACTIVITY TYPE field blank.

Alex moved on to enter fixed cost for the following cost elements (see Figure 5.9):

- ▶ 405200 Office supplies use
- ▶ 430000 Salaries
- ▶ 435000 Annual bonus
- ▶ 470101 Meals
- ▶ 473000 Postage

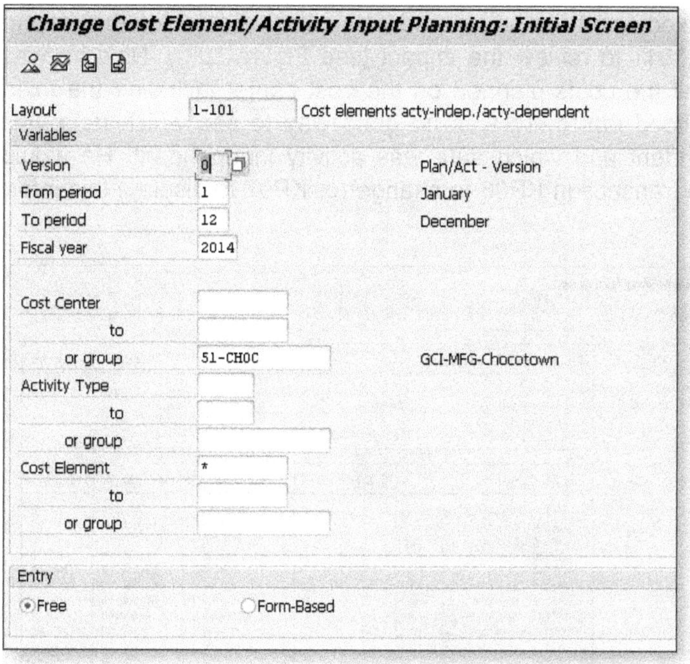

Figure 5.8: KP06 — Initial activity independent cost planning screen

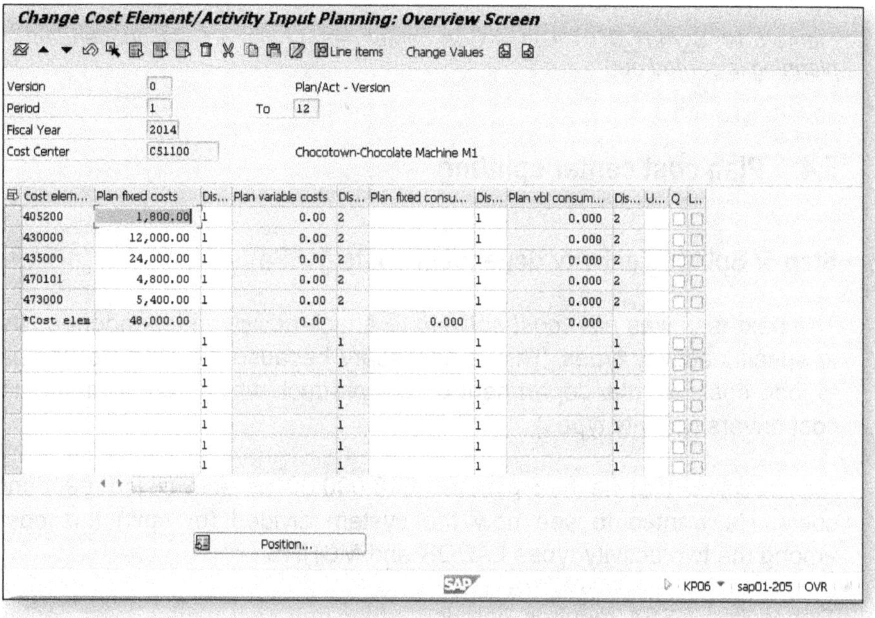

Figure 5.9: KP06 — Overview of activity independent cost planning screen

Once the fixed cost was entered, he went back to the report S_ALR_87013611 to review the impact (see Figure 5.10). Now he was able to see all the costs planned on the cost center including the fixed costs. He noticed that there was no good way to see which data was activity dependent and which data was activity independent. He would need to go to transaction KP06 to change (or KP07 to display) this information.

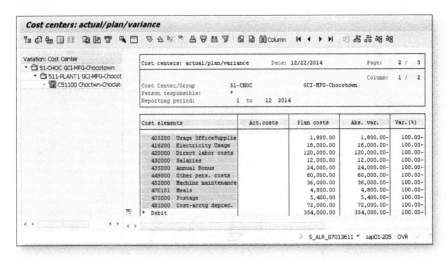

Figure 5.10: S_ALR_87013611 — Cost center report (after activity independent planning is carried out)

5.4 Plan cost center splitting

Step 5: Splitting activity dependent costs (KSS4)

The next task was *plan cost splitting* to attach activity independent costs to specific activity types. This is necessary because the ultimate goal is to load costs for this department on the product, which can be done via cost drivers (activity types).

Alex recalled that he had planned $48,000.00 as activity independent costs. He wanted to see how the system divided (or split) this cost among the two activity types LABOR and MCHRS.

Transaction KSS4 requires entering either one cost center, cost center group, selection variant (a predefined list of cost centers), or all cost centers (see Figure 5.11). Additionally, version, year, and period information also need to be provided. Last, the system provides options for background processing (for performance reasons, especially if the data set is large), test run (to review data before posting it for good), and detail lists.

The menu path is as follows: ACCOUNTING • CONTROLLING • COST CENTER ACCOUNTING • PLANNING • ALLOCATIONS • SPLITTING.

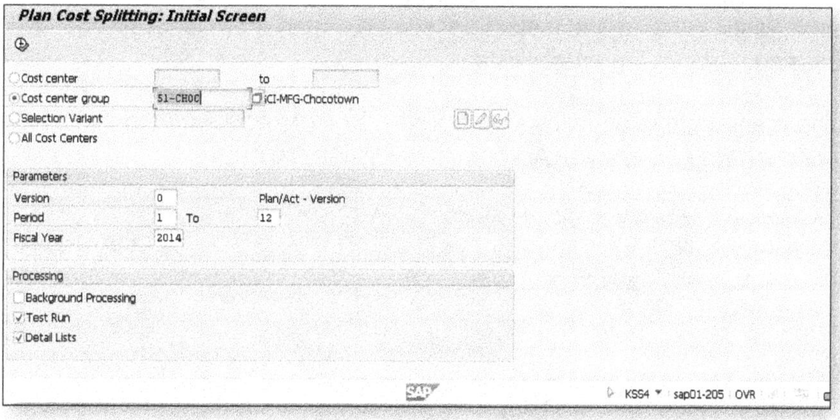

Plan Cost Splitting: Initial Screen

○ Cost center		to
● Cost center group	51-CHOC	☐ iCI-MFG-Chocotown
○ Selection Variant		
○ All Cost Centers		

Parameters

Version	0	Plan/Act - Version
Period	1 To	12
Fiscal Year	2014	

Processing

☐ Background Processing
☑ Test Run
☑ Detail Lists

KSS4 ▾ sap01-205 OVR

Figure 5.11: KSS4 — Plan cost splitting initial screen

Once Alex hit the EXECUTE button on the top-left corner of the initial screen in KSS4, he was brought to the detail list screen (see Figure 5.12) where he noticed that the activity independent plan amount of $48,000.00 was split evenly between the activity types LABOR and MCHRS. As no splitting rules were maintained, the system divided the costs equally. However, it is possible to split this cost in the ratio of quantities between the two activity types if desired.

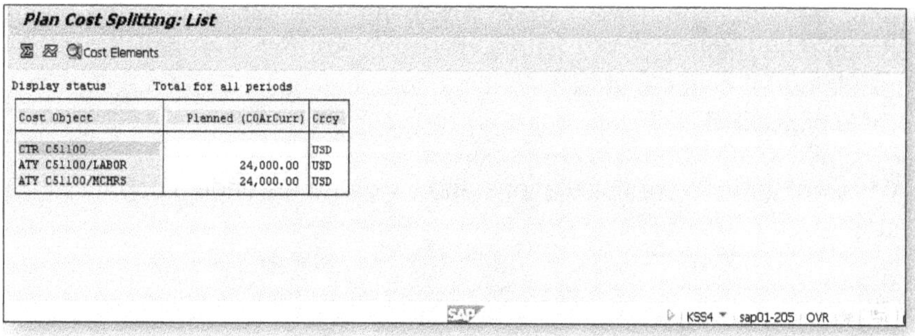

Plan Cost Splitting: List

☒ ☒ ☖ Cost Elements

Display status   Total for all periods

Cost Object	Planned (COArCurr)	Crcy
CTR C51100		USD
ATY C51100/LABOR	24,000.00	USD
ATY C51100/MCHRS	24,000.00	USD

KSS4 ▾ sap01-205 OVR

Figure 5.12: KSS4 — Plan cost splitting result screen

5.5 Plan activity price calculation

Step 6: Activity price calculation (KSPI)

The last step in cost center planning is *plan activity price calculation,* achieved by running transaction KSPI. Similar to other planning transactions, Alex noted various fields such COST CENTER GROUP, VERSION, PERIOD, and YEAR in the selection screen, apart from background processing, test run, and detail lists.

The menu path is as follows: ACCOUNTING • CONTROLLING • COST CENTER ACCOUNTING • PLANNING • ALLOCATIONS • PRICE CALCULATION.

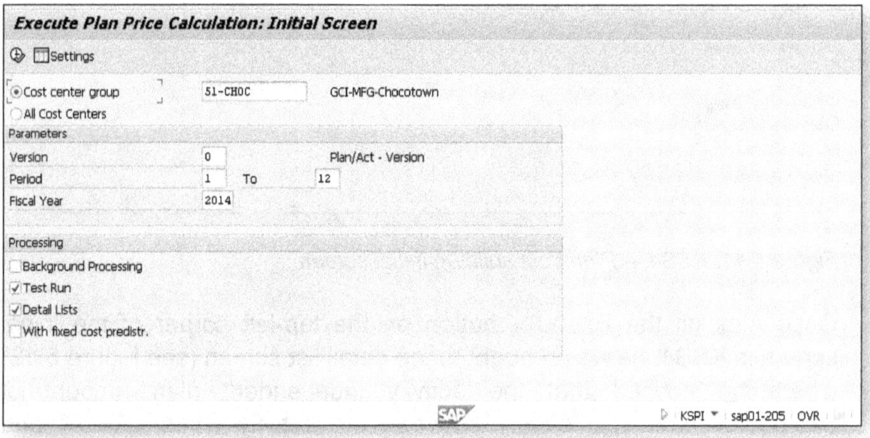

```
Execute Plan Price Calculation: Initial Screen
⊕  ☐Settings

⊙ Cost center group        51-CHOC          GCI-MFG-Chocotown
○ All Cost Centers
Parameters
Version                    0                Plan/Act - Version
Period                     1      To    12
Fiscal Year                2014

Processing
☐ Background Processing
☑ Test Run
☑ Detail Lists
☐ With fixed cost predistr.

                                   SAP          ▷  KSPI ▼  sap01-205  OVR
```

Figure 5.13: KSPI — Plan price calculation initial screen

Once Alex hit the EXECUTE button on the top-left corner of the initial screen in KSPI (see Figure 5.13), he was brought to the detail screen (see Figure 5.14) where he noticed that the activity prices calculated for cost center/activity type combinations C51100/LABOR and C51100/MCHRS.

Alex went through the calculations and validated his understanding of the numbers in KSPI.

Activity Type LABOR had a total activity dependent cost of $180,000.00 (entered in KP06) for 6,000 planned hours (entered in KP26), bringing the activity rate to $30.00/hr. Additionally, the activity independent cost of $24,000.00 was determined (in KSS4 cost splitting), thereby increasing the rate by $4.00/hr. The total cost of LABOR was $34.00/hr. of which, the fixed component was $4.00.

Activity type MCHRS had a total activity dependent cost of $128,000.00 (entered in KP06) for 1,800 planned hours (entered in KP26), bringing the activity rate to $70.00/hr. Additionally, an activity independent cost of $24,000.00 was determined (in KSS4 cost splitting), thereby increasing the rate by $13.33/hr. The total cost of LABOR was $83.33/hr. of which, the fixed component was $73.33. Alex noticed that the system showed a fixed price for MCHRS as $7,333.33 – with a "price unit" or 100. This was done to avoid rounding differences.

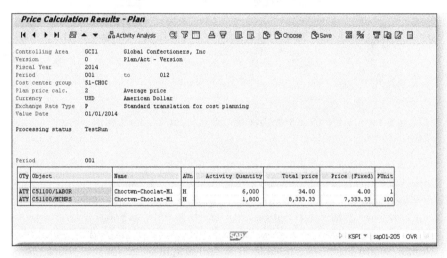

Figure 5.14: KSPI — Plan price calculation result screen

Alex now wanted to see the final impact of the plan price calculation step in the report. He jumped over to S_ALR_87013611 to note that now the credit side of the plan costs were populated with the respective amounts attributable to the two activity types (see Figure 5.15). The net amount of debits minus credits was zero. This means the cost center plan was fully absorbed.

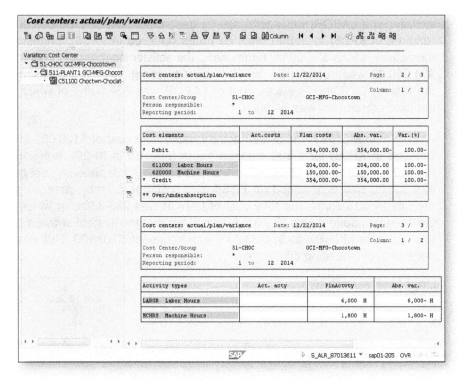

Figure 5.15: S_ALR_87013611 — Cost center report (after activity price calculation is carried out)

Alex took a final look at his example in the spreadsheet (see Figure 5.16) and was impressed by the way this played out in the system. Of course, his example only involved one cost center and a handful of cost elements for simplicity purposes, but he wanted to prove the concept and ensure that he understood the dependencies from one step to another. No doubt, when there are multiple cost centers involved for the entire plant, as well as multiple cost elements for each of the cost centers, the planning process becomes very complex. This is where the system's functionalities can be relied upon.

Cost Element	Description	Activity	Quantity (Hours)	Amount ($) Variable	Fixed	Total	Rate ($ / Hr) Variable	Fixed	Total
420000	Direct labor costs	LABOR		120,000.00		120,000.00			
449000	Other pers. costs	LABOR		60,000.00		60,000.00			
		KP26	6,000	180,000.00	0.00	180,000.00	30.00	0.00	30.00
						KP06			
452000	Machine maintenance	MCHRS			36,000.00	36,000.00			
481000	Cost-acctg deprec.	MCHRS			72,000.00	72,000.00			
416200	Electricity Usage	MCHRS		18,000.00		18,000.00			
		KP26	1,800	18,000.00	108,000.00	126,000.00	10.00	60.00	70.00
						KP06			
405200	Usage OfficeSupplies				1,800.00	1,800.00			
430000	Salaries				12,000.00	12,000.00			
435000	Annual Bonus				24,000.00	24,000.00			
470101	Meals				4,800.00	4,800.00			
473000	Postage				5,400.00	5,400.00			
		*		0.00	48,000.00	48,000.00			
						KP06			
	Cost Splitting	LABOR			24,000.00	24,000.00	0.00	4.00	4.00
		MCHRS			24,000.00	24,000.00	0.00	13.33	13.33
						KSS4			
	Price Calculation	LABOR		180,000.00	24,000.00	204,000.00	30.00	4.00	34.00
		MCHRS		18,000.00	132,000.00	150,000.00	10.00	73.33	83.33
				198,000.00	156,000.00	354,000.00			
									KSPI

* These costs were planned on the Production Line Cost Center to simplify this example. These costs can also be planned on Support Cost Centers and then flow via Plan Assessment (KSUB) or / and Plan Distribution (KSVB).

Figure 5.16: Cost center planning example snapshot from spreadsheet

5.6 Plan allocations

During his orientation, Alex learned about GCI's Chocotown manufacturing facility, which was divided into two plants. Plant-specific costs were captured in their respective cost centers. However, there were certain costs that were captured in common cost center C51900.

Costs captured in the common cost center were allocated to plant-specific cost centers using distributions and assessments.

Distribution is an allocation process in which the original primary cost element is carried over from the sender to the receiver. However, in the case of *assessment*, the cost allocation takes place using a secondary cost element. In other words, the identity of the cost element is lost using an assessment.

GCI uses a combination of both distribution and assessment in its planning and actual process, so two transaction codes were involved.

KSUB – Plan distribution

Menu path: ACCOUNTING • CONTROLLING • COST CENTER ACCOUNTING • PLANNING • ALLOCATIONS • DISTRIBUTION

KSVB – Plan assessment

Menu path: ACCOUNTING • CONTROLLING • COST CENTER ACCOUNTING • PLANNING • ALLOCATIONS • ASSESSMENT

Alex also came across various tools for cost center planning. He listed them down in a small table (see Figure 5.17) for reference.

Steps for Planning on Cost Centers at GCI			
Description of transaction	Create / Change	Purpose	Display
Set Planner Profile	KP04	Provides combination of fields suitable for your planning needs	
Activity Quantity Planning	KP26	Planning of activity quantity for the planning period	KP27
Activity Dependent Cost Planning	KP06	Planning of activity dependent (direct) costs	KP07
Activity Independent Cost Planning	KP06	Planning of activity independent (indirect / overhead) costs	KP07
Plan Cost Center Splitting	KSS4	Attach Activity Indepdent costs to specific Activity Types	
Plan Activity Price Calculation	KSPI	Calculate predetermined absorption rate (burden rate)	

Tools for Cost Center Planning		
Description of transaction	Transaction code	Purpose
Direct input of activity prices	KP26	Activity type rates are fed manually, instead of being calculated via KSPI - Plan Price Calculation
Mass Upload of Activity Quantities	KP26	Upload activity quantities using a comma separated (csv) text file
Quantity data from long term planning	KSPP	Transfers Long Term Planning (LTP) data to cost centers (Activity Quantity input via KP26 can be avoided or reduced)
Mass Upload of Planned Costs	KP06	Upload costs using a comma separated (csv) text file
Copy from previous year's plan	KP97	Previous year's plan is the base for upcoming year's plants
Copy from previous year's actuals	KP98	Previous year's actual is the base for upcoming year's plants
Plan Cost Distribution	KSVB	Allocation of costs (sender cost element retained)
Plant Cost Assessment	KSUB	Allocation of costs (sender cost element not available)
Activity Price Report	KSBT	Report of Activity prices for cost center /cost center group

Figure 5.17: Planning steps and tools for cost center planning

6 Absorption: Aren't cost centers like a sponge?

> "I kind of like to be a sponge, in a way. So everywhere that I am, I like to keep an open mind and just get ideas from everything."
> —Bethany Mota

Now that the plan for the upcoming year is complete, it is time to look at how actual costs are booked and absorbed at cost center level. Cost centers collect costs throughout a month and then pass along some of the costs during the month and at the end of the month. The process of collecting and passing along costs is called *absorption*.

6.1 Actual cost booking

Not all costs end up in cost centers. There are certain costs that are recorded as other cost objects, for example, production order, process order, internal orders, work breakdown structure (WBS) elements, and product cost collectors. Those costs that are directly attributable to a cost object and will be booked on the cost object, such as a raw material consumed during manufacturing, will be consumed at the process order level. A raw material consumed for a specific purpose of a trial will be consumed at an internal order level. Labor hours spent erecting a new set of machinery that will be used for production can be charged to a WBS element. A cost center, however, is usually the most common sender/receiver of costs in a manufacturing setup.

Examples of cost center postings in a manufacturing facility are:

▶ A production line cost center typically receives the wage costs of shop floor staff dedicated to that particular production line, as well depreciation of machinery that makes up the production line.

▶ A maintenance cost center receives costs related to spare parts consumed for regular maintenance.

> ▶ An energy cost center receives costs related to power, steam, and other utilities consumed for the plant.

> ▶ A common cost center for the plant receives costs for a plant manager's salary and all other common costs that a plant incurs.

The following is an example that illustrates the flow of costs in cost center report S_ALR_87013611.

Figure 6.1 shows that several cost elements had actual postings to cost center C511000, including cost element 404000 (spare parts) in the amount of $200.00.

The menu path is as follows: ACCOUNTING • CONTROLLING • COST CENTER ACCOUNTING • INFORMATION SYSTEM • PLAN/ACTUAL COMPARISONS • COST CENTERS: ACTUAL/PLAN/VARIANCE.

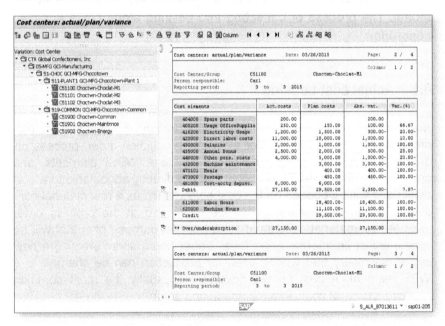

Figure 6.1: S_ALR_87013611 — Actual cost booking on production line cost center

Figure 6.2 shows that cost center C51901 had a posting of $2,000.00 for cost element 404000 (spare parts) and $6,000.00 for cost element 452000 (machine maintenance).

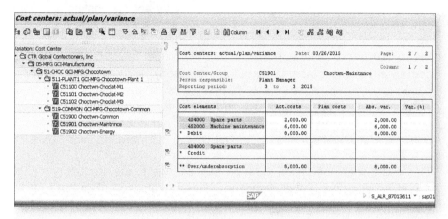

Figure 6.2: S_ALR_87013611 — Actual cost booking on maintenance cost center

6.2   Activity absorption

A product carries the costs of material, labor, and overhead that were used for its manufacturing. The material cost can be more or less tangible and identifiable with the inputs. But labor, and overhead measurement are usually based on the number of hours spent on manufacturing the product. Effectively, it is the *conversion cost* for making the product, or the cost of converting a raw material into a semi-finished material, or a semi-finished material into a finished material.

Plan activity prices are calculated during the planning phase. These prices are nothing more than predetermined absorption rates that will be used for each activity type unit. Effectively, if the activity price for direct labor is $30.00/hour and the machine hour is $120.00/hour, then a product that consumes two hours of direct labor and three hours of machine hours will carry $60.00 absorption of direct labor and $360.00 of absorption of machine hours. At this time, the process order gets debited for the cost of $420.00 and the cost center gets credited. It is this credit that provides absorption, whereas the debits provide the actual cost.

Now it is very likely that that the actual cost debit on the cost center will not be equal to what was absorbed in the cost center. The difference is called *over/under absorption* (see Figure 6.3). In other words, perfect absorption (no under/over absorption) purely by activity posting is a very rare situation.

There could be several reasons for over/under absorption, including *spending variance* (spent more than planned), *volume variance* (produced less than planned or activity quantity was less than planned), *mix variance* (mix or types of products produced were different than planned), or *efficiency variance* (labor was too fast and consumed fewer labor hours, or machines were too slow and consumed more machine hours).

This over/under absorption must be passed over to the product (via KSII actual activity price calculation and CON2 revaluation of orders), or to another cost center (by way of a cost center to cost center allocation KSU5/KSV5), or to profitability segment (by way of cost center to CO-PA allocation KEU5), or a combination of all of above.

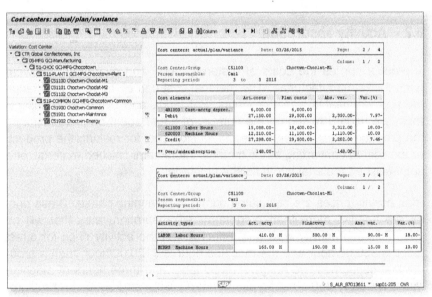

Figure 6.3: S_ALR_87013611 — Activity absorption on production line cost center

6.3   Actual allocations

Apart from the costs booked directly at the cost center level, such as wages and depreciation, a production line cost center will receive costs from various other cost centers in the plant. Some of the examples of cost center allocations are:

▶ Maintenance costs from a maintenance cost center (the most commonly used drivers are machine hours across various production line cost centers).

▶ Energy costs from an energy cost center (production volume across various production line cost centers can be used as the basis of allocation. If there are meters installed in each department that allow tracking of actual energy consumption, then an accurate allocation can be made using statistical key figures, or in the allocation cycle).

▶ Support staff costs such as plant manager's salary, finance costs, IT costs, warehouse costs, R&D costs, and quality costs (here too, production volume across various production line cost centers can be used as the basis of allocation).

Costs can be allocated using distribution (transaction KSV5 where original cost element is used to allocate costs), or assessments (transaction KSU5—a secondary cost element known as assessment cost element is used to allocate costs). Other methods include template allocation (transaction KPAS) and actual cost reposting (KB11N).

Figure 6.4 shows transaction KSV3 with SEGMENT HEADER of DISTRIBUTION CYCLE MAINT visible. 100% of ACTUAL VALUES will be allocated in the proportion of ACTUAL ACTIVITY

The menu path is as follows: ACCOUNTING • CONTROLLING • COST CENTER ACCOUNTING • PLANNING • ALLOCATIONS • DISTRIBUTION • EXTRAS • CYCLE • DISPLAY.

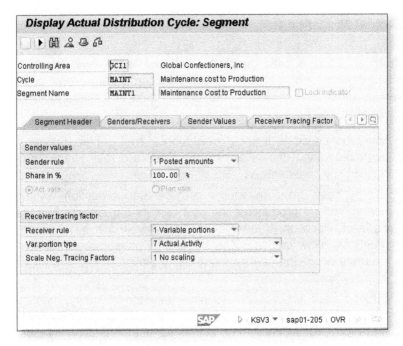

Figure 6.4: KSV3—Distribution MAINT segment header

Figure 6.5 shows the SENDER/RECEIVER tab where the SENDER COST CENTER C51901 will send costs incurred in COST ELEMENT GROUP ALL to the RECEIVER COST CENTER GROUP "511-PLANT1".

This would mean that cost center C51901 (Chocotown-Maintenance) will transfer all costs to cost center group 511-PLANT1, which includes following cost centers:

- ▶ C51100 Chocotown-Chocolate Machine M1
- ▶ C51101 Chocotown-Chocolate Machine M2
- ▶ C51102 Chocotown-Chocolate Machine M3

Figure 6.6 shows the RECEIVER TRACING FACTOR tab where ACTIVITY TYPE MCHRS (machine hours) will be used to proportionately allocate the costs to receiver cost centers.

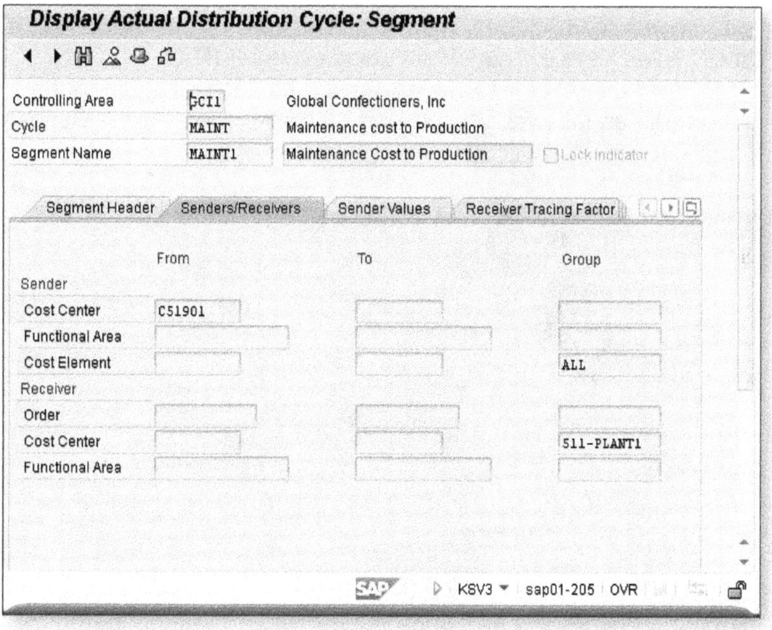

Figure 6.5: KSV3 — Distribution MAINT sender receiver

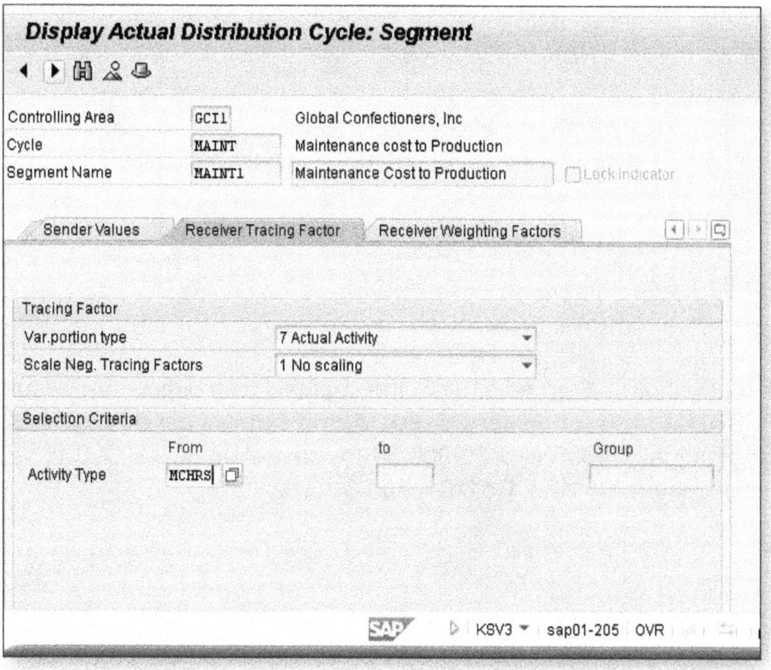

Figure 6.6: KSV3 — Distribution MAINT receiver tracing factor

Figure 6.7 shows EXECUTE ACTUAL DISTRIBUTION (transaction KSV5) where three cycles were executed, including cycle MAINT.

The menu path is as follows: ACCOUNTING • CONTROLLING • COST CENTER ACCOUNTING • PLANNING • ALLOCATIONS • DISTRIBUTION.

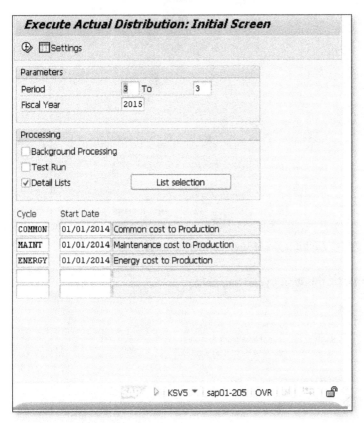

Figure 6.7: KSV5 — Distribution execute

Figure 6.8 shows the result of the actual distribution in report S_ALR_87013611. Cost center C51901 distributed its cost of $2,000.00 for cost element 404000 and $6,000.00 for cost element 452000 to receiver cost centers C51100, C51101, and C51102.

P	Segment	Cost Elem.	O...	Object	OTy	Obje	PTy	Partner object	Σ	Val/COArea Crcy
3	MAINT1	404000	C...	C51100			C...	C51901		1,047.62
	MAINT1	404000	C...	C51901			C...	C51100		1,047.62-
	MAINT1	404000	C...	C51101			C...	C51901		444.44
	MAINT1	404000	C...	C51901			C...	C51101		444.44-
	MAINT1	404000	C...	C51102			C...	C51901		507.94
	MAINT1	404000	C...	C51901			C...	C51102		507.94-
	MAINT1	452000	C...	C51100			C...	C51901		3,142.86
	MAINT1	452000	C...	C51901			C...	C51100		3,142.86-
	MAINT1	452000	C...	C51101			C...	C51901		1,333.33
	MAINT1	452000	C...	C51901			C...	C51101		1,333.33-
	MAINT1	452000	C...	C51102			C...	C51901		1,523.81
	MAINT1	452000	C...	C51901			C...	C51102		1,523.81-
									*	0.00
									**	0.00

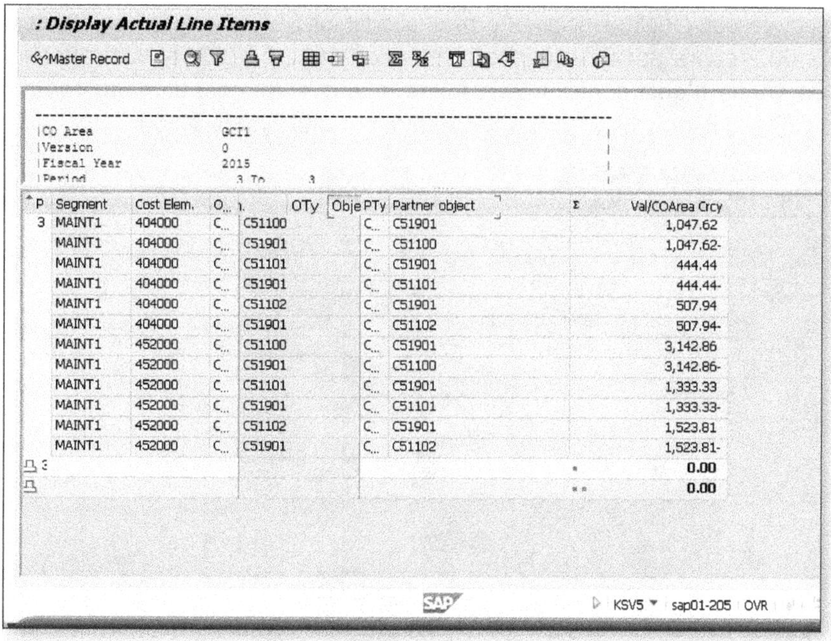

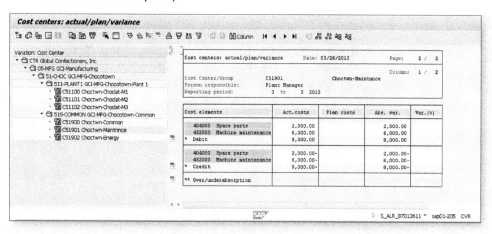

Figure 6.8: KSV5—Distribution results

Figure 6.9 shows the cost in C15901 is now full absorbed (there is no over/under absorption).

Cost centers: actual/plan/variance Date: 03/26/2015 Page: 2 / 2
Column: 1 / 2
Cost Center/Group C51901 Choctwn-Maintnnce
Person responsible: Plant Manager
Reporting period: 3 to 3 2015

Cost elements	Act.costs	Plan costs	Abs. var.	Var.(%)
404000 Spare parts	2,000.00		2,000.00	
452000 Machine maintenance	6,000.00		6,000.00	
* Debit	8,000.00		8,000.00	
404000 Spare parts	2,000.00-		2,000.00-	
452000 Machine maintenance	6,000.00-		6,000.00-	
* Credit	8,000.00-		8,000.00-	
** Over/underabsorption				

Figure 6.9: S_ALR_87013611—Maintenance cost center after actual allocations

Cost center C51100 originally had a cost of $200.00 for cost element 404000 (spare parts). After the distribution of $1,047.62 for cost element 404000 from cost center C51901, the total cost for cost element 404000 in C51100 is now $1,247.62 (see Figure 6.1 and Figure 6.10).

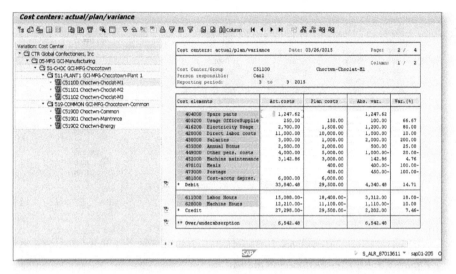

Figure 6.10: S_ALR_87013611 — Production line cost center after allocation

6.4   Actual cost center splitting

Similar to plan cost center splitting, *actual cost center splitting* attaches activity independent costs to a specific activity. Costs associated with a specific cost element (or a cost element group) can be attached to an activity using splitting rules maintained in the splitting structure (transaction OKES) and assignment of cost centers to splitting structure (transaction OKEW).

6.4.1   Splitting structure

The menu path is as follows: TOOLS • CUSTOMIZING • IMG • SPRO EXE-CUTE PROJECT • CONTROLLING • COST CENTER ACCOUNTING • ACTUAL POST-INGS • PERIOD-END CLOSING • ACTIVITY ALLOCATION • SPLITTING • DEFINE SPLITTING STRUCTURE.

Figure 6.11 shows the SPLITTING STRUCTURE "GC" for ASSIGNMENT line "LAB" (Labor) where all costs in COST ELEMENT GROUP "SPLIT_LAB" are attached to ACTIVITY TYPE "LABOR".

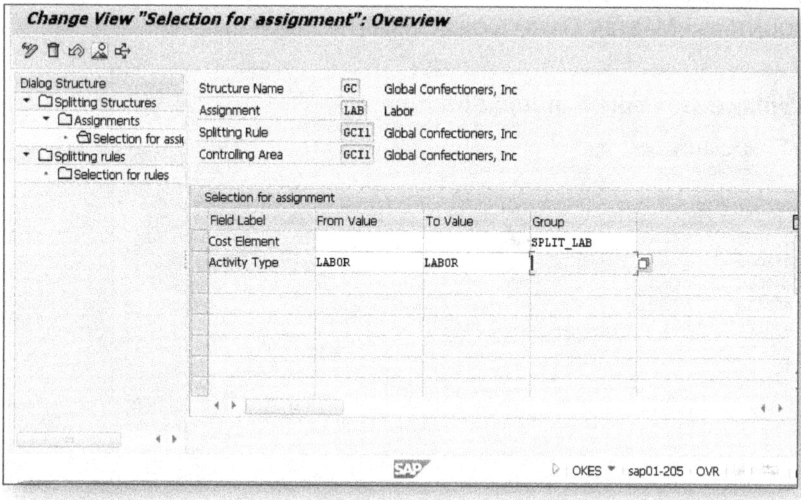

Figure 6.11: OKES — Splitting structure setup for labor

Similarly, Figure 6.12 shows the SPLITTING STRUCTURE "GC" for ASSIGN-MENT line "MCH" (machine hours) where all costs in COST ELEMENT GROUP "SPLIT_MCH" are attached to ACTIVITY TYPE "MCHRS".

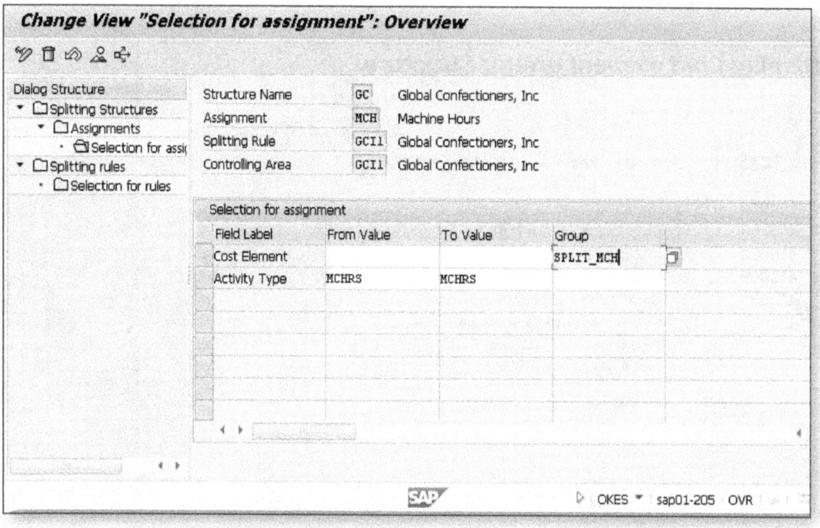

Figure 6.12: OKES — Splitting structure setup for machine hours

The definition of cost element group "SPLIT_LAB" is shown in Figure 6.13 (transaction KAH3).

The menu path is as follows: ACCOUNTING • CONTROLLING • COST CENTER ACCOUNTING • MASTER DATA • COST ELEMENT GROUP • DISPLAY.

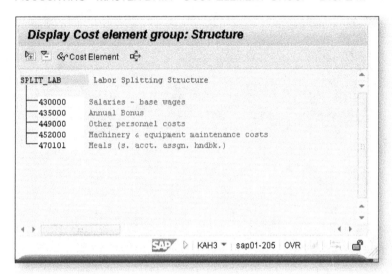

Figure 6.13: KAH3 — Cost element group for splitting labor

Definition of cost element group "SPLIT_MCH" is shown in Figure 6.14 (transaction KAH3).

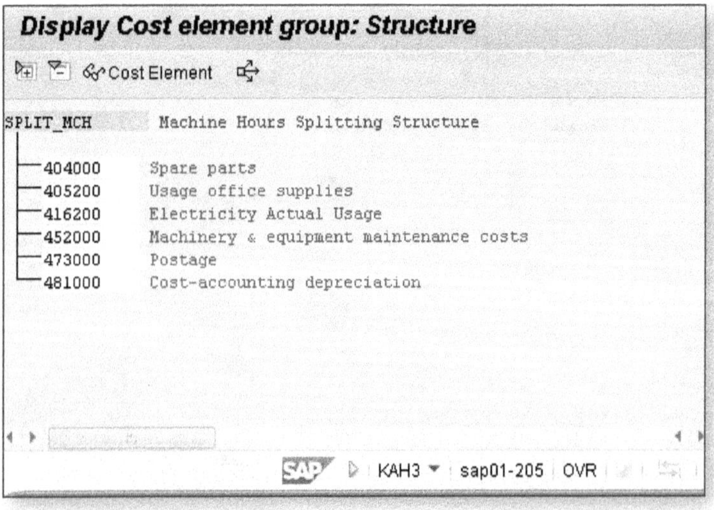

Figure 6.14: KAH3 — Cost element group for splitting machine hours

6.4.2 Assignment of cost centers to splitting structure

Cost centers are attached to a specific splitting rule (OKEW) (see Figure 6.15).

The menu path is as follows: TOOLS • CUSTOMIZING • IMG • SPRO EXECUTE PROJECT • CONTROLLING • COST CENTER ACCOUNTING • ACTUAL POSTINGS • PERIOD-END CLOSING • ACTIVITY ALLOCATION • SPLITTING • ASSIGN SPLITTING STRUCTURE TO COST CENTERS.

All production line cost centers are attached to splitting structure GC. Common cost centers or sending cost centers are not mapped to the splitting structure. In other words, cost centers that are associated with an activity type and have a plan/actual price calculated need to be assigned to a spitting structure.

Both OKES and OKEW are part of a configuration setup that should not change very often.

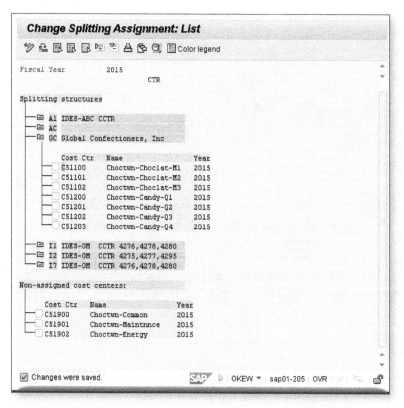

Figure 6.15: OKEW—Assignment of cost centers to splitting structure

6.4.3 Actual cost splitting

Actual cost splitting is performed during month-end close by running transaction KSS2.

The menu path is as follows: ACCOUNTING • CONTROLLING • COST CENTER ACCOUNTING • PERIOD-END CLOSING • SINGLE FUNCTIONS • SPLITTING.

Figure 6.16 shows the ACTUAL COST SPLITTING (KSS2) INITIAL SCREEN. Splitting can be performed at the cost center or cost center group level.

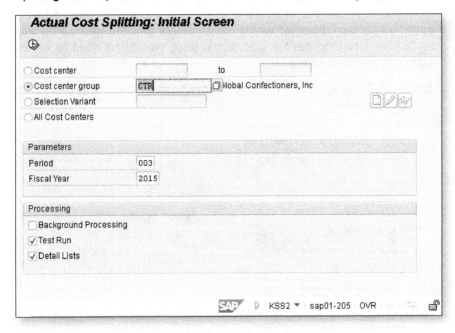

Figure 6.16: KSS2 — Actual cost splitting

Figure 6.17 shows the ACTUAL COST SPLITTING (KSS2) results screen. Cost element group and activity price combinations are maintained in splitting rules (OKES) and cost element groups (KAH3) are used during splitting.

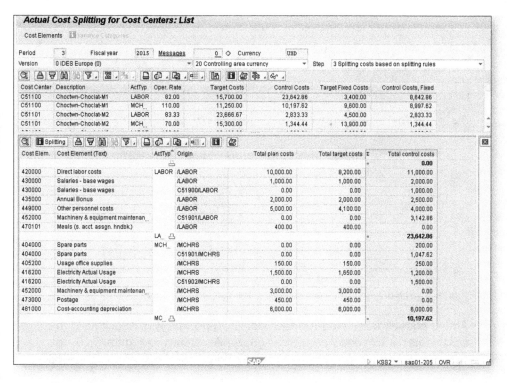

Figure 6.17: KSS2 — Actual cost splitting results

6.5 Actual activity price calculation

Once a link between an activity independent cost and an activity type via cost center splitting is established, you are ready to perform the *actual activity price calculation* using transaction KSII. Price calculation can be performed only at the cost center group level; it cannot be performed at the individual cost center level (see Figure 6.18).

The menu path is as follows: ACCOUNTING • CONTROLLING • COST CENTER ACCOUNTING • PERIOD-END CLOSING • SINGLE FUNCTIONS • PRICE CALCULATION.

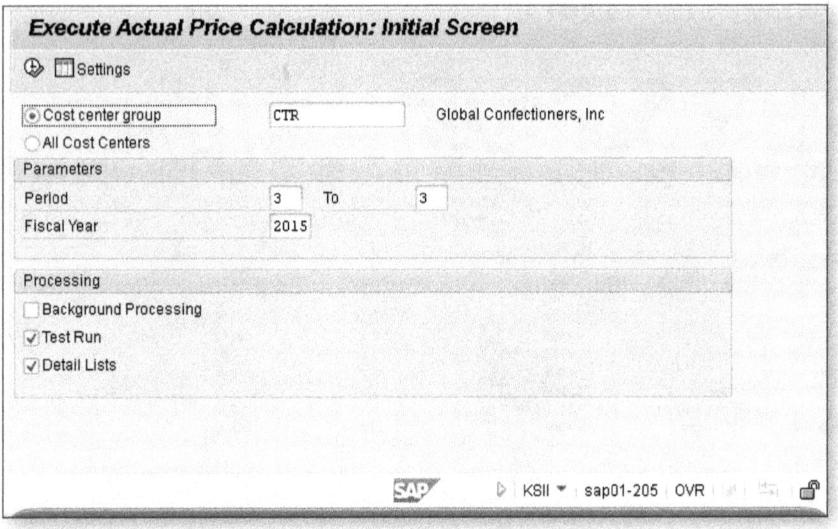

Execute Actual Price Calculation: Initial Screen

⊕ ▥ Settings

- ⦿ Cost center group | CTR | Global Confectioners, Inc
- ○ All Cost Centers

Parameters

| Period | 3 | To | 3 |
| Fiscal Year | 2015 | | |

Processing

- ☐ Background Processing
- ☑ Test Run
- ☑ Detail Lists

Figure 6.18: KSII — Initial actual activity price calculation screen

Actual price is calculated for each activity type that was attached to the cost center within the cost center group. As shown in Figure 6.19, the actual activity price was calculated for activity types LABOR and MCHRS for three production line cost centers C51100, C51101, and C51102. Price units of 10, 100, 1,000, or 10,000 are used to reduce rounding errors.

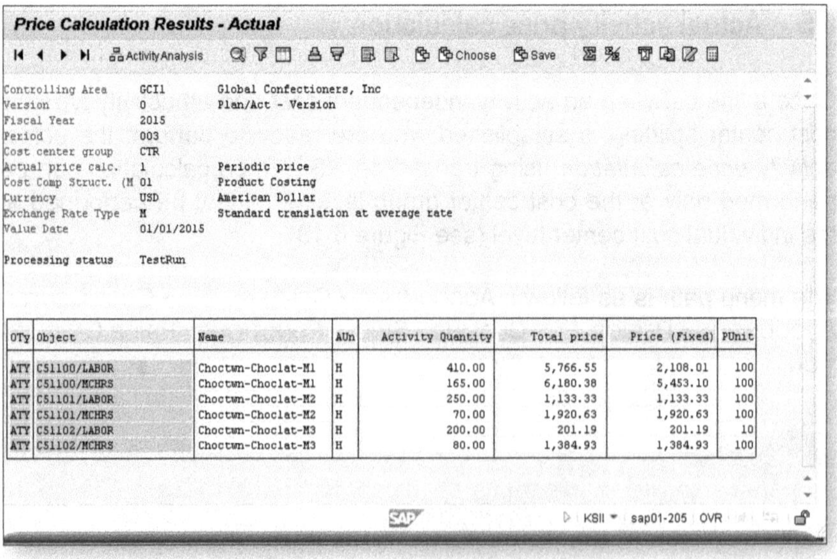

Price Calculation Results - Actual

◄ ◄ ► ► ⛁ Activity Analysis   ⦿ ▽ ▥ ⚏ ▽ ▦ ▦ ⚏ ⚏ Choose ⚏ Save   ⅀ ‰ ▽ ▧ ▨ ▦

Controlling Area	GCI1	Global Confectioners, Inc
Version	0	Plan/Act - Version
Fiscal Year	2015	
Period	003	
Cost center group	CTR	
Actual price calc.	1	Periodic price
Cost Comp Struct. (M	01	Product Costing
Currency	USD	American Dollar
Exchange Rate Type	M	Standard translation at average rate
Value Date	01/01/2015	

Processing status   TestRun

OTy	Object	Name	AUn	Activity Quantity	Total price	Price (Fixed)	PUnit
ATY	C51100/LABOR	Choctwn-Choclat-M1	H	410.00	5,766.55	2,108.01	100
ATY	C51100/MCHRS	Choctwn-Choclat-M1	H	165.00	6,180.38	5,453.10	100
ATY	C51101/LABOR	Choctwn-Choclat-M2	H	250.00	1,133.33	1,133.33	100
ATY	C51101/MCHRS	Choctwn-Choclat-M2	H	70.00	1,920.63	1,920.63	100
ATY	C51102/LABOR	Choctwn-Choclat-M3	H	200.00	201.19	201.19	10
ATY	C51102/MCHRS	Choctwn-Choclat-M3	H	80.00	1,384.93	1,384.93	100

Figure 6.19: KSII — Actual activity price calculation results

6.6 Revaluation of activities on orders

Using transaction CON2, the system will post the difference between the plan rate and the actual rate and revalue the orders with the actual rate at month end. This transaction will provide additional postings to the cost center on the credit side and effectively fully absorb the cost center.

The menu path is as follows: ACCOUNTING • CONTROLLING • PRODUCT COST CONTROLLING • COST OBJECT CONTROLLING • PRODUCT COST BY ORDER • PERIOD-END CLOSING • SINGLE FUNCTIONS • REVALUATION AT ACTUAL PRICES • COLLECTIVE PROCESSING.

Figure 6.20 shows the initial screen for revaluation of orders at actual activity prices. This transaction is executed at plant level.

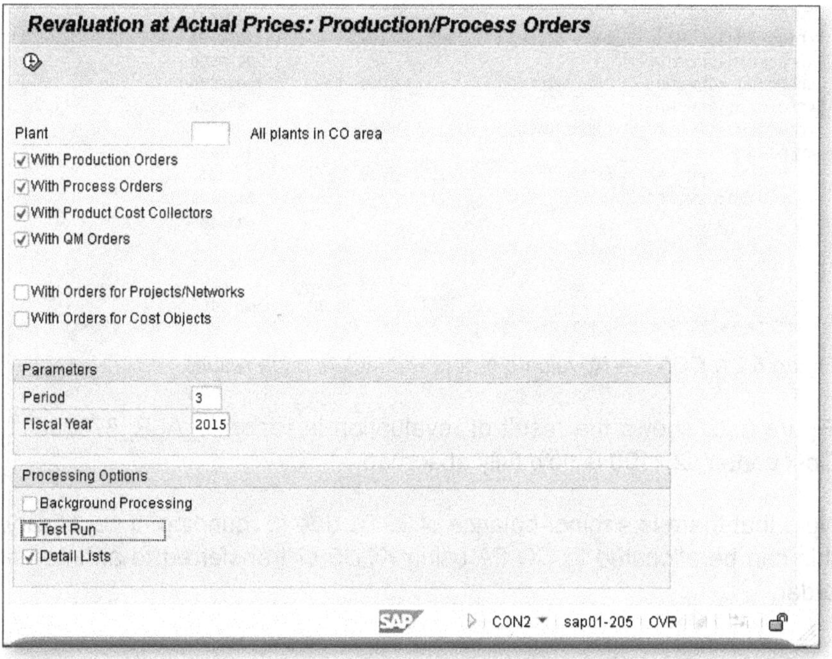

Figure 6.20: CON2 — Revaluate orders with actual price initial screen

Figure 6.21 shows the result of the revaluation. Output provides SENDERS (cost center and activity type combination), RECEIVER (order number), COST ELEMENT, and VALUE IN CONTROLLING AREA CURRENCY (amount of revaluation). Orders 70000742 and 70000743 were revalued with activity

LABOR in the amount of $8,554.86 and MCHRS in the amount of $(2,012.37). The total revaluation for the cost center was $6,542.49.

This revaluation amount matches the unabsorbed amount of $6,542.48 for cost center C51100 as shown in Figure 6.10.

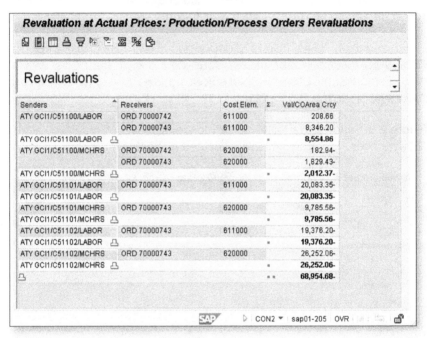

Figure 6.21: CON2— Revaluate orders with actual price results

Figure 6.22 shows the result of revaluation in report S_ALR_87013611. Cost center C51100 is now fully absorbed.

Note that there is a minor balance of $0.01 due to rounding. If necessary, this can be allocated to CO-PA using KEU5 or transferred to an internal order.

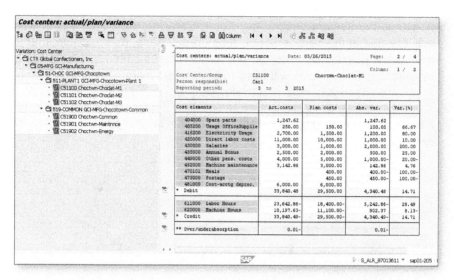

Figure 6.22: S_ALR_87013611 — Production line cost center after revaluation at actual price

Figure 6.23 shows the result of the revaluation in report S_ALR_87013611. All cost centers are now fully absorbed.

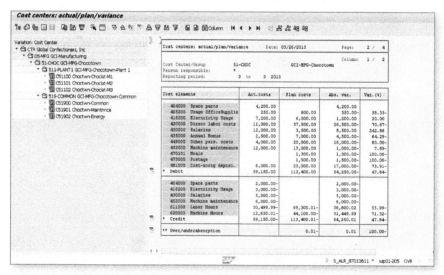

Figure 6.23: S_ALR_87013611 — All cost centers after revaluation at actual price

At times, the system design may necessitate that not all cost elements are included in the cost center splitting. In that case, those cost elements will not be passed along to the production/process/internal orders using revaluation. These costs will need to be cleared manually using a journal entry or an assessment to profitability segment using transaction KEU5.

Alex made note of important transactions in a table (see Figure 6.24) for reference.

Cost Center Absorption Transactions used at GCI		
Description of transaction	Transaction code	Purpose
Actual Cost Distribution	KSV5	Allocation of costs (sender cost element retained)
Actual Cost Assessment	KSU5	Allocation of costs (sender cost element not available)
Maintain Splitting Structure	OKES	Configure Splitting Structure (Cost Elements, Groups, Activities)
Assign cost centers to splitting structure	OKEW	Configure assignment of cost centers to splitting structure
Actual Cost Center Splitting	KSS2	Attach Activity Indepdent costs to specific Activity Types
Actual Activity Price Calculation	KSII	Calculate actual absorption rate (burden rate)
Revaluation at Actual Prices	CON2	Revalues process / production orders with actual activity price

Other transactions		
Description of transaction	Transaction code	Purpose
Cost Centers: Actual/Plan/Variance Report	S_ALR_87013611	Cost Center Report (Amount, Activities, SKFs) - Plan vs Actual
Activity Price Report	KSBT	Report of Activity prices for cost center /cost center group
Cost Center Display	KS03	Display of Cost Center used in Allocation Cycles
Cost Center Group Display	KSH3	Display of Cost Center Group used in Allocation Cycles
Cost Element Display	KA03	Display of Cost Element used in Allocation Cycles
Cost Element Group Display	KAH3	Display of Cost Element Group used in Allocation Cycles
Activity Type Display	KL03	Display of Activity Type used in Allocation Cycles
Statistical Key Figure (SKF) Display	KK03	Display of SKF used in Allocation Cycles

Figure 6.24: Cost center absorption transactions used at GCI

7 Product costs: Where do all the direct costs end up?

"In the beginning God created man ... and the costs followed afterwards."
—Profound Patricia, Management Accountant

Product costing is the valuation of material components and activities on a process or production order utilizing material prices and activity rates. Plan and actual values are recorded and reported with variances and variances are disposed of according to company policy. Product costing is where all the direct costs for a product end up. The indirect costs in this context are sales, general, and administrative (SG&A in common terms) expenses that are usually not absorbed into the product costs.

From the perspective of inventory valuation, a manufacturing unit should include all of the costs of raw materials and conversion costs, including any overhead that went into manufacturing a finished product.

7.1 Product costing drivers

The user manual listed the following drivers for product costing:

- ▶ Material quantities are derived (read) from the bill of material (BoM or BOM).
- ▶ The components are costed as per costing method (standard or moving/weighted average), by reading the values stored in the material masters, purchasing information records (PIRs), or some other planned price valuation method like trending (historical average) price.
- ▶ The activities are costed by applying activity rates as the product moves through the routing (or recipe in the case of process industry) or operations performed in the work centers (resources in case of process industry) in the manufacturing facility.

► Overhead costs are absorbed into the product cost via activity types and/or costing sheet.

7.2 Master data dependencies

BOM and routing (or recipe) are commonly referred to as *quantity structure*, meaning quantities for costing will be read from these master data elements. As you know, BOM requires the material master to be setup, whereas routing (or recipe) requires a work center (or resource) to be setup.

A BOM uses the material master to fetch component material quantities and uses PIRs or other planned prices to fetch rates at which materials will be costed.

A routing (or recipe) uses work center (or resource) to fetch activity quantities. Activity prices are maintained for a specific combination of activity type and cost center using cost center planning.

For raw materials or procured semi-finished or finished materials, the price as per material master or PIR is used during costing. *Valuation variant* determines the access sequence of prices (which price should be used first, whether PIR or standard price from the material master, or moving average price from material master).

If a recipe uses an activity type for setup time, then the costing lot size used during costing will have an impact on the setup cost per unit. A larger costing lot size would result in a smaller setup cost per unit. In contrast, a smaller costing lot size would provide a higher setup cost per unit.

The training manual spoke at length about various production master data, specifically material master, BOM, work center (resource), and routing (recipe). Even though these master data elements are not owned or always maintained by finance or product costing teams, they are an integral part of SAP ERP. These master data elements provide very powerful integration between production process and product costing.

7.3 Material master

Material master (or simply material) is an alphanumeric key that identifies a material. A material can be a raw material, semi-finished material, finished material, or a spare part. Material depicts a physical or logical grouping with the same form, fit, and function. Use of material master is fundamental to goods movement. Material and its use spans across multiple SAP modules as well as processes in an organization. Once transactions are posted, it is very difficult to change some of these fields without significant rework. Therefore, material definition is very important at an early stage of an SAP implementation.

A material can be displayed using transaction MM03. Because there can be multiple uses of a material, a material master is defined with views that are logically grouped together by functions or process areas. Some of the views in a material master include: BASIC DATA; MRP; WORK SCHEDULING; GENERAL PLANT DATA / STORAGE; ACCOUNTING; COSTING, etc.

The menu path is as follows: LOGISTICS • MATERIALS MANAGEMENT • MATERIAL MASTER • DISPLAY • DISPLAY CURRENT.

7.3.1 Fields that impact product costs and are owned by finance

Accounting 1/Costing 2

Figure 7.1 shows an example of fields in the ACCOUNTING 1/COSTING 2 view of the material master.

Valuation class provides a link between the material master and FI. Valuation class facilitates posting of the stock values of materials of the same material types to the same GL accounts.

Price control refers to the method of *inventory valuation*. SAP Controlling offers two methods of inventory valuation and product costing: STANDARD COST (indicator "S") and MOVING/WEIGHTED AVERAGE (indicator "V"). This is identified at the material master level, thus different materials can use different valuation methods within a plant. However, finished and semi-finished materials which are produced in-house must always use the "S" indicator. Procured items can use "S" or "V" depending on corporate policy/project decision.

Standard versus moving average price control

 Finished and semi-finished materials produced in-house must always use the standard cost "S" indicator. Procured items can use "S" or "V" depending on corporate policy/project decision.

The *standard price* (or standard cost) field stores the price for the material. Price should be expressed in per price unit per base unit of measure in the given currency (for example, USD 4,590/1,000 KG; EUR 2,961.29/1,000 KG). If a material is valued per moving average price control, then the value in standard price field is statistical in nature, that is, this field is not used in recording goods movement transactions.

Price unit prevents rounding issues while carrying out goods movement transactions.

Use of price unit

 A material priced at 29.37 cents, or $0.2937 each should be created with a price unit of at least 100, so that the price is $29.37/100 or even better, $293.70/1,000. Doing so will prevent rounding differences.

The *material ledger active* indicator signifies if the material ledger is active for this plant. The flag is automatically set when the material ledger is activated for that plant.

The *price determination* indicator applies only when the material ledger is used for that plant. It establishes the rules for rolling up costs in the material ledger — single-level (material-specific) or multi-level (rolled-up cost of components to produced materials).

Moving average price is the price at which the material is valuated. The valuation of stocks at moving average price means that the price of the material is adjusted to reflect the continual fluctuations in the procurement price. If a material is valued as per standard price control, then the value in moving the average price field is statistical in nature, that is, this field is not used in recording goods movement transactions.

Valuation category is used when *split valuation* is activated. It is an indicator that determines whether stocks for the material are valuated together or separately. If the valuation category is maintained, as with a batch indicator, then the material is valued at the *batch* level, that is, each individual batch will have its own cost. If the valuation category is blank, then all batches are valued with the same cost. This indicator also determines which valuation types are allowed, that is, the criteria by which stocks can be valuated.

Valuation type is the individual value below material level. This field is only used when split valuation is activated; when each batch is a valuation type. If a material is valued as per origin, domestic or imported, then each origin is a valuation type.

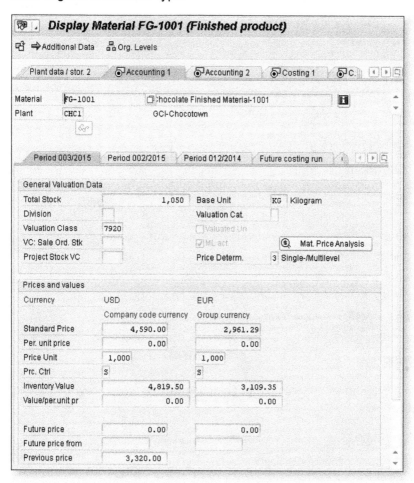

Figure 7.1: MM03 — Accounting1 view

Accounting 2

Figure 7.2 has an example of fields in the ACCOUNTING 2 view of material master

TAX PRICE 1 is the price at which the material is valuated for tax valuation purposes. This price can be determined with different standard cost estimates or can be set manually.

COMMERCIAL PRICE 1 is the price at which the material is valuated for commercial valuation purposes. This price can be determined with different standard cost estimates or can be set manually.

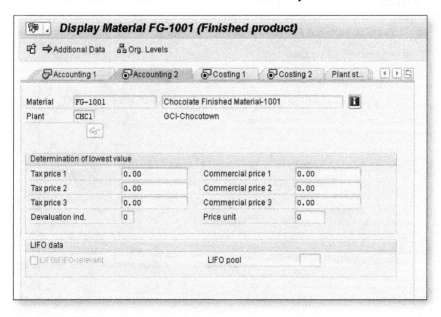

Figure 7.2: MM03 — Accounting 2 view

Costing 1

Figure 7.3 shows an example of fields in the COSTING 1 view of material master.

Do not cost indicator controls whether a cost estimate can be created for a material. Material is not costed if this indicator is checked.

Origin groups are used to break costs down below a cost component level. The origin groups are assigned to a cost component so that costing can be viewed at this level.

The *with quantity structure* indicator improves performance at the time of structure explosion during costing.

The *material origin* indicator helps to analyze material costs during reporting by providing material number detail.

Variances can only be calculated for the orders for which a *variance key* has been maintained. All produced materials must have a variance key. One standard value should be defined for the variance key.

The *overhead group* is a key that defines which overhead basis/formula will be applied to the material while carrying out standard cost estimate.

Overhead group for freight

Overhead group of 10% freight on raw materials, 8% freight on packaging materials, and 3% cost on other supplies can be set up to include estimated freight in standard costs.

The *profit center* field identifies the responsible department, location, or a product line of a business unit—depending on the profit center design implemented. Profit center on the material will be derived on transactional data including process order, purchase order, and sales order.

The *costing lot size* is the quantity used for cost estimates. The costing lot size must be the same or greater than the price unit on the accounting screen.

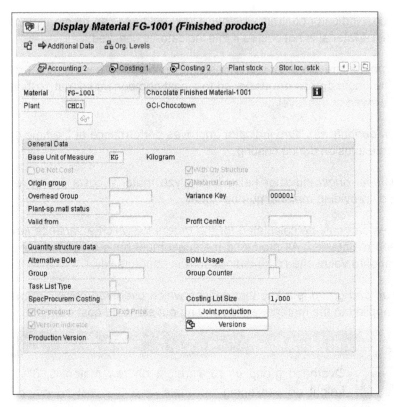

Figure 7.3: MM03 — Costing 1 view

Costing 2

Figure 7.4 shows an example of the fields in the COSTING 2 view of material master.

The marked cost estimate is stored in the *future planned price* field. This field is updated when the "mark cost estimate" step is performed in transaction CK24/CK40N, it cannot be updated directly in the material master.

The released cost estimate is stored in the *current planned price* field (the value in this field is also updated in the *standard price* field). Both of these fields are updated during the "release cost estimate" step in transaction CK24/CK40N and cannot be updated directly in material master.

The previously released cost estimate is stored in the *previous planned price* field. This field is updated when a new cost estimate is released. Similar to future and current planned price, this field cannot be updated directly in the material master.

Updating cost estimates in the material master

 Future, current, and previous planned price fields cannot be updated directly in the material master. They are updated when the cost estimate mark/release step is performed in transaction CK24/CK40N.

Planned price 1 is a manually set price that can override other prices if configured in the valuation variant access sequence.

Planned price date 1 is the date from which the planned price is effective (relevant to valuation date in costing run).

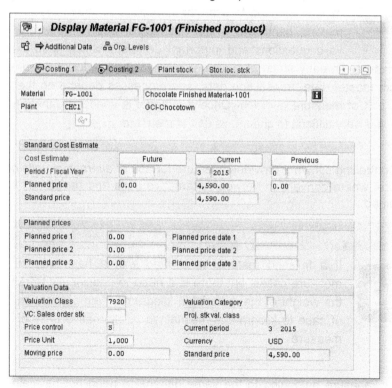

Figure 7.4: MM03 — Costing 2 view

7.3.2 Fields not directly owned by finance, but impact product costs

Basic data 1

Figure 7.5 shows an example of fields in the COSTING 2 view of the material master.

Base unit of measure is what unit the cost will be expressed in, in the costing and accounting views. The base unit of measure that will be used requires careful deliberation at the design stage because it cannot be changed once maintained and dependent transactions are carried out.

Base unit of measure decision

Should finished products like chocolate bars be maintained in grams, kilograms, or by the case? Should aluminum foil used to wrap the chocolate be maintained in meters, centimeters, feet, inches, or both? These are valid questions and important decisions which need to be made at an early stage of system implementation. A lot of downstream master data, transaction data, and processes depend on the base unit of measure decision. Once a material is used for transactions, it is very difficult to change its unit of measure.

SAP Controlling software provides a feature for use of *alternative units of measure*, where conversion between alternative units and based unit is maintained.

Alternative units of measure

If a finished material is created with a base unit of measure cases, but there is a need to additionally track the weight of the material in kilograms, then conversion of case to kilogram is maintained in alternative units of measure

Units of measure belonging to the same dimension need not be maintained in alternative units. As an example, if a material is created with a base unit of measure of kilograms, there is no need to maintain conversion from kilograms to grams at the material master level. The system will automatically derive the conversion as 1,000 grams to a kilogram since both these belong to the dimension 'mass.' However, a conversion of this material from kilograms to cubic feet or cubic meters will need to maintained as an alternative unit, given that cubic feet and cubic meters belong to the dimension 'volume.'

Material status is used to determine which transactions are allowed for the given material status. *Cross-plant material status* maintained in the BASIC DATA view applies to all plants. *Plant-specific material status* in the plant views (MRP1 and COST 1) override the status in the BASIC DATA view.

Product hierarchy is an alphanumeric character string used to structure product characteristics, for example, AA-BBB-CCCC-DD-E. Product hierarchy design has an impact on CO-PA and sales reporting.

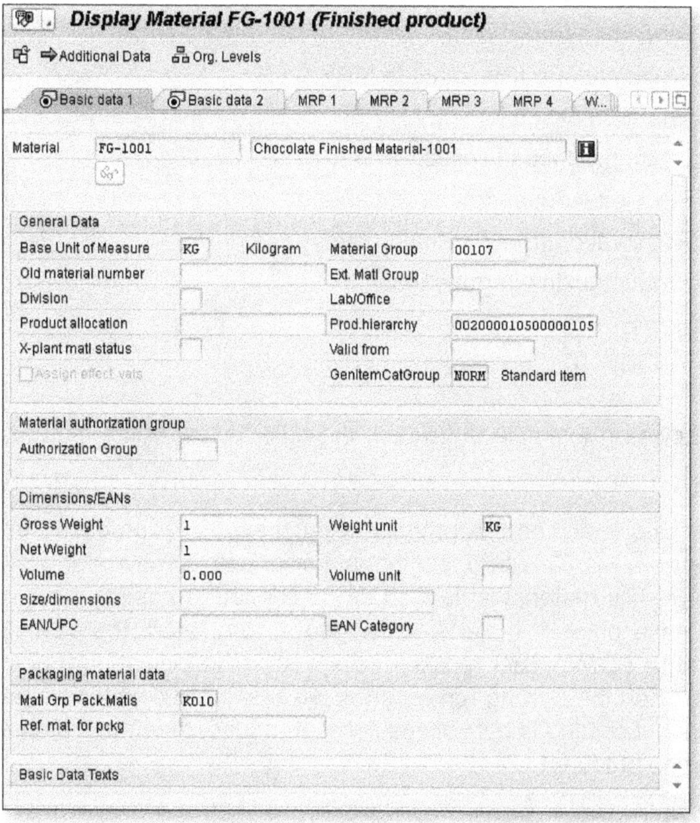

🐷 .	Display Material FG-1001 (Finished product)	

🗄 ⇒ Additional Data   ⛁ Org. Levels

| ⊙ Basic data 1 | ⊙ Basic data 2 | MRP 1 | MRP 2 | MRP 3 | MRP 4 | W... |

| Material | FG-1001 | Chocolate Finished Material-1001 | ℹ |

General Data

Base Unit of Measure	KG	Kilogram	Material Group	00107
Old material number			Ext. Matl Group	
Division			Lab/Office	
Product allocation			Prod.hierarchy	00200010500000105
X-plant matl status			Valid from	
☐ Assign effect vals			GenItemCatGroup	NORM	Standard item

Material authorization group

| Authorization Group | |

Dimensions/EANs

Gross Weight	1		Weight unit	KG
Net Weight	1			
Volume	0.000		Volume unit	
Size/dimensions				
EAN/UPC			EAN Category	

Packaging material data

| Matl Grp Pack.Matls | K010 |
| Ref. mat. for pckg | |

Basic Data Texts

Figure 7.5: MM03 — Basic data 1 view

99

MRP2/Costing 1

The *materials requirement planning* (MRP) view is important from a planning standpoint. There are a few fields that influence costing.

Material status is used to determine which transactions are allowed for a particular material status. CROSS PLANT MATERIAL STATUS maintained in the *basic data* view applies to all plants. PLANT-SPECIFIC MATERIAL STATUS in the plant views (*MRP1* and *Cost 1*) override the status in the basic data view.

SPECIAL PROCUREMENT KEY (SPK) 30 is used for sub-contracting. Options in special procurement key include:

- ▶ 10 Consignment
- ▶ 20 External procurement
- ▶ 30 Subcontracting
- ▶ 40 Stock transfer (procurement from alternate plant)
- ▶ 45 Stock transfer from plant to MRP area
- ▶ 50 Phantom assembly
- ▶ 52 Direct production/collective order
- ▶ 60 Planned independent requirements
- ▶ 70 Reservation from alternate plant
- ▶ 80 Production in alternate plant

MRP2

Figure 7.6 shows an example of fields in the MRP2 view of the material master.

Procurement type indicates if a product is purchased (F), produced in-house (E), or both (X). This field is important from both MRP and a costing perspective. If a material is flagged as purchased, a costing run will look for purchase price. If material is flagged as produced, the costing run will look for a BOM/master recipe for the cost. If the indicator for both is maintained, then the costing run program will first try to cost the material as in-house. If costing is not successful as in-house, then the material will be costed as procured.

The *backflush* indicator can be set in the material master. It influences whether a component material will be issued directly (the exact quantity consumed will be entered explicitly) or defaulted from a BOM standard. Two indicators are possible for backflush:

1. Always backflush.

2. Work center decides whether to backflush.

If option 1 is selected, then the default value in the BOM will be used for consumption. If maintained as option 2 or left blank, then the backflush rule can be set at the individual routing/recipe stage.

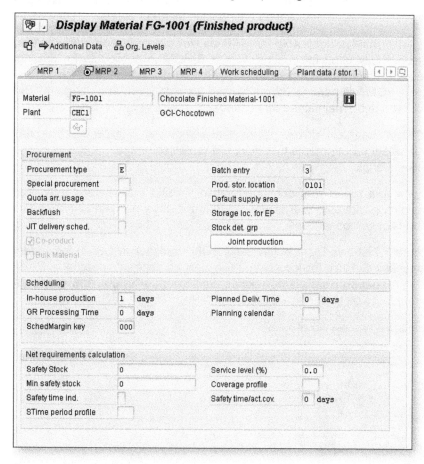

Figure 7.6: MM03 — MRP2 view

7.4 Bill of material

A *bill of material* is a detailed list of components needed to make up a semi-finished good (SFG) or finished good (FG). The list contains the object number, quantity, and unit of measure of each component. The components are known as BOM items.

A product can be manufactured using one or more different BOMs due to different production methods. Each set of BOMs is called an *alternative BOM*.

Bills of materials are plant-specific (where the same finished material can be produced using different components in different plants).

USAGE 1 BOM is applicable for MRP, as well as production, and can also be optionally used for costing. USAGE 6 BOM is applicable for costing. Keeping different BOM usages implies dual maintenance (such as, usage 1 BOM will need to be maintained for production and usage 6 BOM will need to be maintained for costing).

BOM for usage 1 drives planning requirements. The demand creates dependent requirements that drive the replenishment of components and bulk materials.

A *phantom material* is contained within a BOM that is not costed and contains no inventory. It is used purely for ease of maintaining certain groups of components.

Figure 7.7 shows DISPLAY MATERIAL BOM (transaction CS03) for header material FG-1001 for which there is one component material - RAW-1001. The menu path is as follows: LOGISTICS • PRODUCTION • MASTER DATA • BILLS OF MATERIAL • BILLS OF MATERIAL • MATERIAL BOM • DISPLAY.

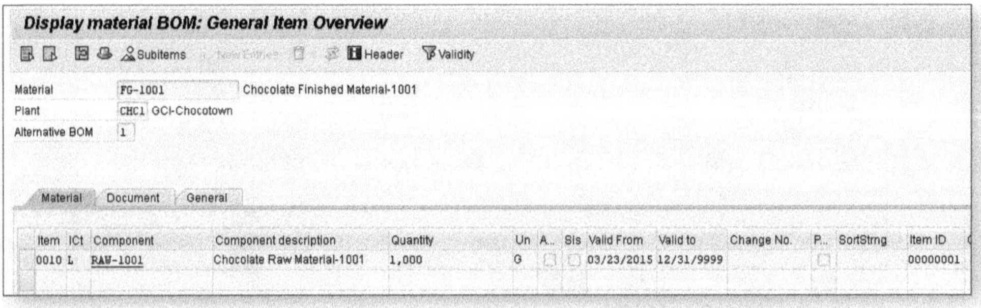

Figure 7.7: CS03 — Bill of material

Figure 7.8 shows the COSTING RELEVANCY flag in the STATUS/LONG TEXT view at the BOM item level.

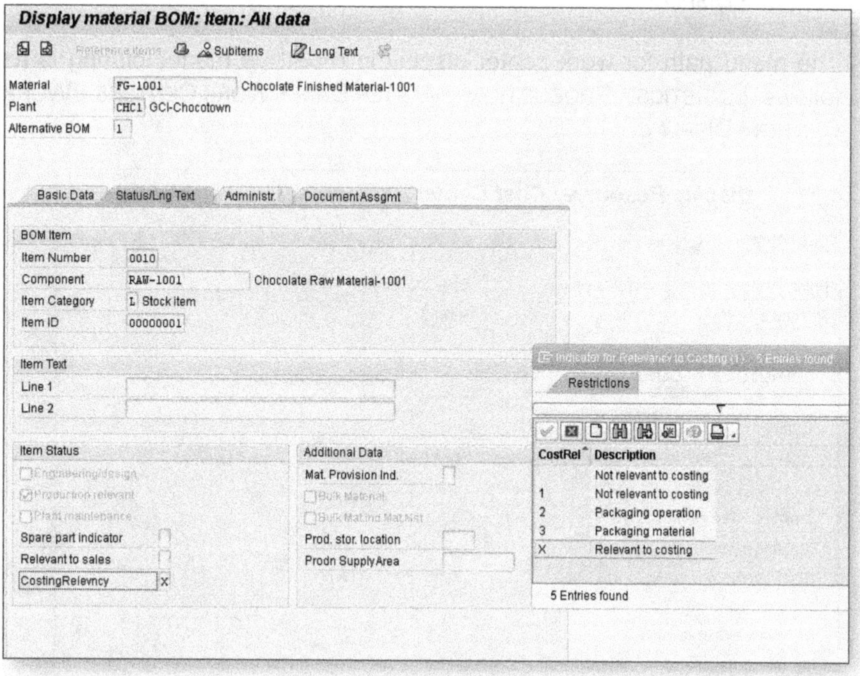

Figure 7.8: CS03 — BOM costing relevancy flag

7.5 Work center/resource

A *resource* (or *work center* in the case of repetitive manufacturing) represents a processing area, individual machine, a group of machines, or an entire production line. Every operational production step is carried out as a production resource. Production resources are created to represent a processing area, individual machine, a group of machines, or an entire production line. Production resources are linked to cost centers to define cost calculation and reporting. Production resources are created at the plant level.

Figure 7.9 shows DISPLAY RESOURCE: COST CENTER ASSIGNMENT (transaction CRC3). Default ACTIVITY TYPES are maintained with a formula for costing.

The menu path for resource display in the process industry is as follows: LOGISTICS • PRODUCTION - PROCESS • MASTER DATA • RESOURCES • RE-SOURCE • DISPLAY.

The menu path for work center display in repetitive manufacturing is as follows: LOGISTICS • PRODUCTION • MASTER DATA • WORK CENTERS • WORK CENTER • DISPLAY.

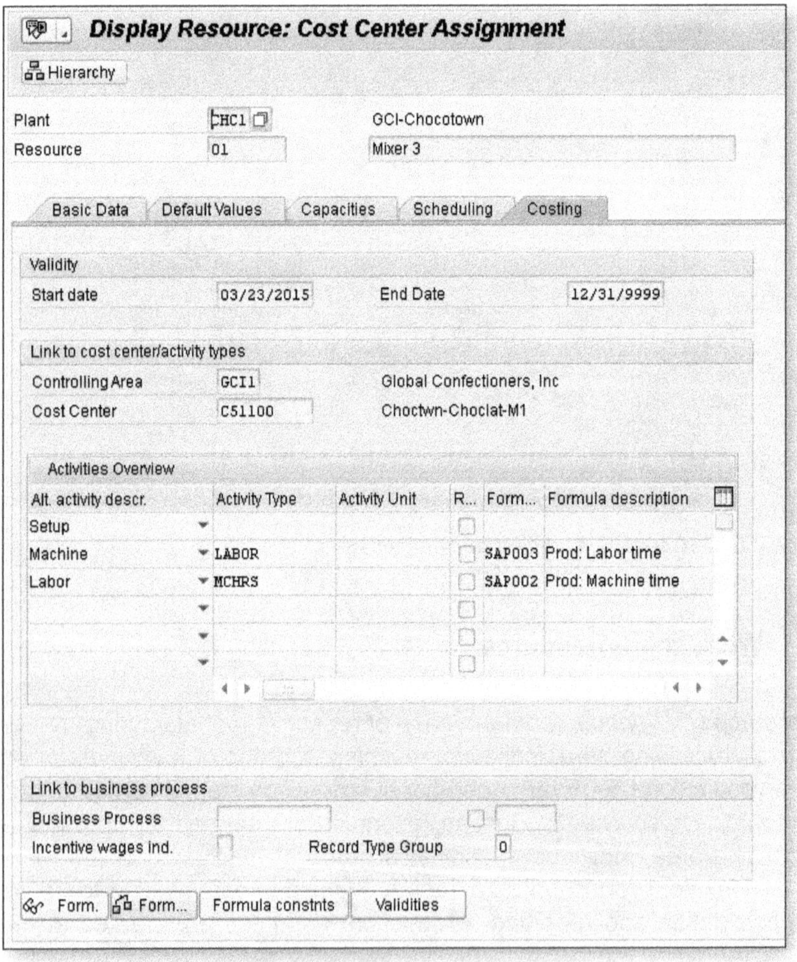

Figure 7.9: CRC3 — Resource costing tab

7.6 Routing/master recipe

A *master recipe* is required for every produced SFG or FG and is a combination of BOM and routings (operation steps). It consists of a header and several operations. Each operation is carried out at a resource.

A production version is used to link a BOM alternative to a routing (operations) so that the master recipe design is complete. This is very important when a product has multiple BOMs and multiple routings.

A recipe has various tabs:

▶ RECIPE HEADER: contains the product name, SKU, valid scalable quantities, and QA requirements (inspection plans).

▶ OPERATIONS: contacts the manufacturing process, setup, check-in materials, fill product, etc., and resource and cost information for each operation.

▶ MATERIALS: BOM – contains material numbers and exact proportions.

▶ ADMINISTRATIVE DATA: enables change control (version, effective dates).

Figure 7.10 shows the DISPLAY MASTER RECIPE (transaction C203) OPERATIONS tab.

The menu path is as follows: LOGISTICS • PRODUCTION - PROCESS • MASTER DATA • MASTER RECIPES • RECIPE AND MATERIAL LIST • DISPLAY.

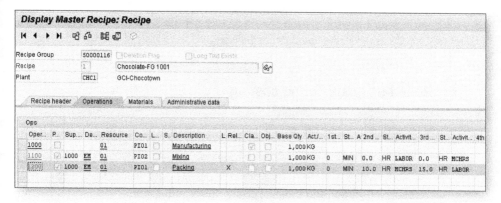

Figure 7.10: C203 — Recipe operations view

Figure 7.11 shows operation details. It takes 10 machine hours and 15 labor hours on RESOURCE 01 to produce 1,000 KG of this product. These hours are represented by activity type. As an example, say that three workers are staffing this machine and there is a plan to staff only two workers. The recipe will need to be updated to reflect this change to 10 hours of labor instead of 15 hours.

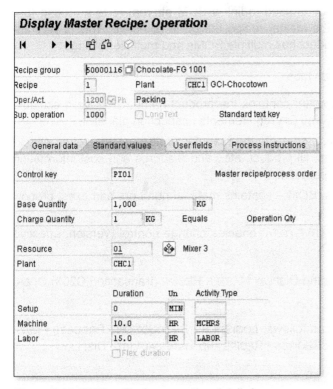

Figure 7.11: C203 — Recipe operation detail view

7.7 Rolled-up costs during costing

Product costing elements are as follows:

▶ Costing variant — determines various strategies for costing.

▶ Activity types — determines which quantity rate will be used for absorbing direct and indirect costs (labor, equipment, etc.).

▶ Cost component — determines how costs will be summarized.

▶ Costing sheet — determines how overhead costs will be added.

▶ Cost estimate — holds planned costs for a material or process order.

▶ Costing run — allows costing of multiple materials at the same time.

7.7.1 Costing variant

The *costing variant* is a repository of certain business rules that contain all control parameters for costing, including parameters that control how cost estimates are executed and the material prices or activity prices that are used to valuate the costing items.

In material costing (costing with and without quantity structure), the costing variant determines the following:

▶ Costing type (where will you use this costing).

▶ Valuation variant (what will be used for costing).

▶ Date control (what dates will be used for valuation and quantity structure).

▶ Quantity structure determination ID (what BOM/master recipe will be used for costing, production, etc.).

▶ Transfer control (whether components will be re-costed, or will pass on their existing roll-up cost).

Figure 7.12 shows COSTING VARIANT configuration setup (transaction OKKN).

The menu path is as follows: TOOLS • CUSTOMIZING • IMG • SPRO EXECUTE PROJECT • CONTROLLING • PRODUCT COST CONTROLLING • PRODUCT COST PLANNING • MATERIAL COST ESTIMATE WITH QUANTITY STRUCTURE • DEFINE COSTING VARIANTS.

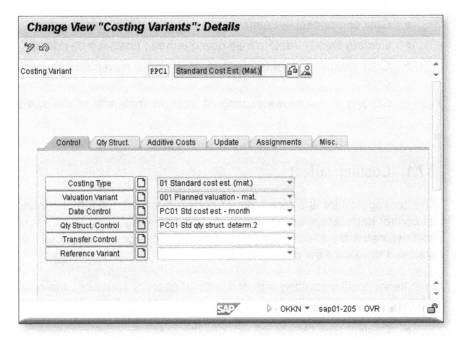

Figure 7.12: OKKN — Costing variant

7.7.2 Valuation variant

Valuation variant defines how the material, activities, subcontractors, and overhead surcharges will be valued using strategy sequences for each, such as first use 1, if it has no value, use 2, etc.

- ▶ Material valuation — price from purchasing info record.
- ▶ Activities — plan price for the period.
- ▶ Subcontractors — net purchase order price.
- ▶ External processing — effective price from quotation.
- ▶ Overhead — costing sheet PP-PC1.

Figure 7.13 shows the VALUATION VARIANT configuration setup (transaction OKK4).

The menu path is as follows: TOOLS • CUSTOMIZING • IMG • SPRO EXECUTE PROJECT • CONTROLLING • PRODUCT COST CONTROLLING • PRODUCT COST PLANNING • MATERIAL COST ESTIMATE WITH QUANTITY STRUCTURE • COSTING VARIANT: COMPONENTS • DEFINE VALUATION VARIANTS.

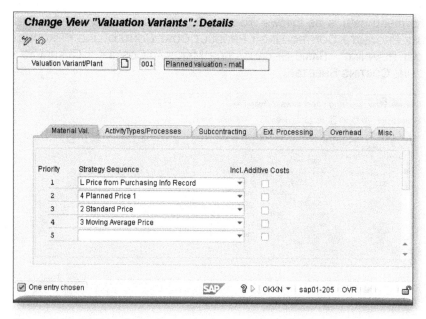

Figure 7.13: OKK4 — Valuation variant

7.7.3 Costing sheet

A *costing sheet* is used to allocate indirect overhead to a product.

A specified percentage of overhead is applied to the product based on material issues or labor activity charges on the production order.

Cost centers with the indirect overheads are credited.

Examples of overhead calculation include:

▶ Inbound freight cost as a percentage of base material cost.

▶ $/kilogram based on weight of material.

▶ $/kilogram based on weight of material for specific origin group.

▶ $/hour based on hours spent (use of overhead rates can give similar results to that of using activity type, but it uses a different vehicle for absorbing costs).

Figure 7.14 shows the COSTING SHEET configuration setup (transaction KZS2).

The menu path is as follows: TOOLS • CUSTOMIZING • IMG • SPRO EXE-CUTE PROJECT • CONTROLLING • PRODUCT COST CONTROLLING • PRODUCT COST PLANNING • BASIC SETTINGS FOR MATERIAL COSTING • OVERHEAD • DEFINE COSTING SHEETS.

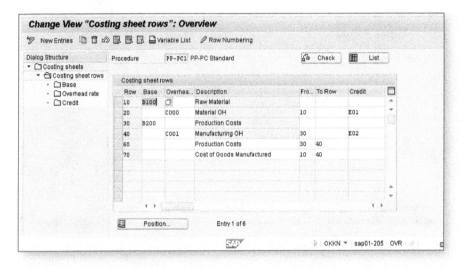

Figure 7.14: KZS2 — Costing sheet

7.7.4 Cost estimate

A *cost estimate* is the planned cost of a production cost carrier. It utilizes the BoM and routing (quantity structure) to arrive at the planned cost, which can be transferred to the material master as a planned price to be utilized in product costing to valuate the material. The costing variant controls which cost estimate should be considered for the standard cost estimate.

Figure 7.15 shows the CREATE MATERIAL COST ESTIMATE WITH QUANTITY STRUCTURE (transaction CK11N) in the COSTING DATA tab.

The menu path is as follows: CONTROLLING • PRODUCT COST CONTROLLING • PRODUCT COST PLANNING • MATERIAL COSTING • COST ESTIMATE WITH QUANTITY STRUCTURE • CREATE.

Figure 7.16 shows CREATE MATERIAL COST ESTIMATE WITH QUANTITY STRUCTURE (transaction CK11N) in the DATES tab.

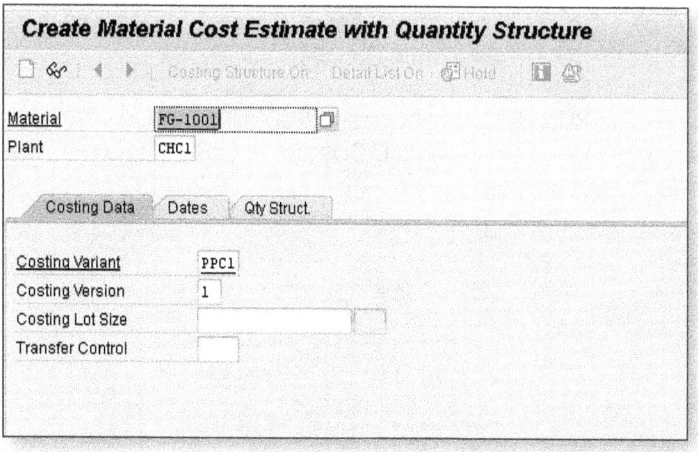

Create Material Cost Estimate with Quantity Structure

Costing Structure On   Detail List On   Hold

Material   FG-1001
Plant   CHC1

Costing Data   Dates   Qty Struct.

Costing Variant   PPC1
Costing Version   1
Costing Lot Size
Transfer Control

Figure 7.15: CK11N— Create cost estimate with quantity structure initial screen

Dates in cost estimate

 COSTING DATE FROM cannot be in the past for a standard cost estimate that is released to material master. Validity dates of BOM and routing/recipe used for costing will depend on QUANTITY STRUCTURE DATE. Material and activity prices will depend on the VALUATION DATE selected in the cost estimate selection screen.

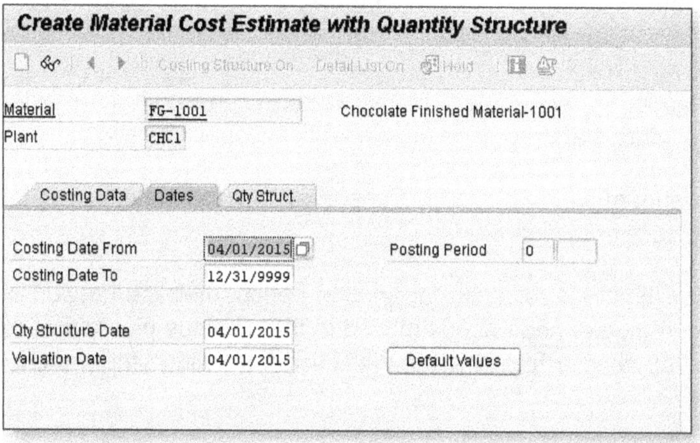

Create Material Cost Estimate with Quantity Structure

Costing Structure On   Detail List On   Hold

Material   FG-1001   Chocolate Finished Material-1001
Plant   CHC1

Costing Data   Dates   Qty Struct.

Costing Date From   04/01/2015   Posting Period   0
Costing Date To   12/31/9999

Qty Structure Date   04/01/2015
Valuation Date   04/01/2015   Default Values

Figure 7.16: CK11N— Create cost estimate with quantity structure dates

Figure 7.17 shows the results of the DISPLAY MATERIAL COST ESTIMATE WITH QUANTITY STRUCTURE (transaction CK13N).

The menu path is as follows: CONTROLLING • PRODUCT COST CONTROLLING • PRODUCT COST PLANNING • MATERIAL COSTING • COST ESTIMATE WITH QUANTITY STRUCTURE • DISPLAY.

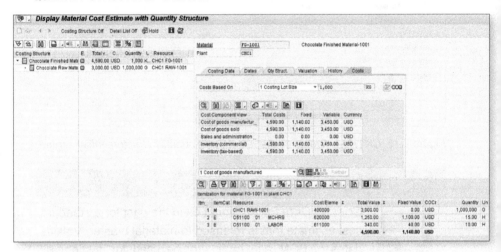

Figure 7.17: CK11N — Create cost estimate with quantity structure results

Once the cost estimate is reviewed and validated for accuracy, cost estimates are MARKED and RELEASED (transaction CK24).

The menu path is as follows: CONTROLLING • PRODUCT COST CONTROLLING • PRODUCT COST PLANNING • MATERIAL COSTING • PRICE UPDATE.

A marked standard cost estimate is transferred to the material master record as the future standard price (costing and accounting view).

A released standard cost estimate is transferred into the material master record as the current standard price.

When a cost estimate is released for another period, then the previously maintained current planned price is moved to the previous planned price field, thereby allowing a historical view of price from within the material master.

Cost estimate release

Releasing an incorrect cost estimate may result in incorrect financial postings. It is not possible to release another cost estimate for the same period unless reorganization is performed. Releasing a new price in the same period is technically not possible if the material ledger is implemented. It is very important that a cost estimate is thoroughly reviewed before releasing the cost.

7.7.5 Costing run

The *costing run* enables you to cost multiple materials at the same time. It reproduces the entire process of costing a product with a BOM. It can be executed in background mode for large volumes of materials.

Costing results can be used to mark and release several standard cost estimates at once. Mark and release steps are built into the CK40N mass costing run (unlike CK11N individual costing where mark and release are performed using another transaction, CK24).

Figure 7.18 shows EDIT COSTING RUN (transaction CK40N).

The menu path is as follows: CONTROLLING • PRODUCT COST CONTROLLING • PRODUCT COST PLANNING • MATERIAL COSTING • COSTING RUN • EDIT COSTING RUN.

Edit Costing Run

☐ ☐ With Reference ✐ ⓐ ⬡

| Costing Run | CHC1_ALL | Description | Chocotown Plant-All Materials | |
| Costing Run Date | 03/29/2015 | | | ✔ |

🗐 General Data
🗁 Create Cost Estimate

Flow Step	Authorization	Parameter	Execute	Log	Status	Materials	Errs	Still Open
Selection		)⬡	⊕		▢	2	0	
Struct. Explosion		)⬡	⊕		▢	2	0	
Costing		)⬡	⊕	⚙	▢	2	0	0
Analysis		)⬡	⊕		▢			
Marking	⛁	)⬡	⊕	⚙	▢	2	0	0
Release		)⬡	⊕	⚙				

🗐 Costing Results

Figure 7.18: CK40N— Costing run

7.8 Cost components

The cost of a product is usually made up of material, labor, overhead, and subcontract costs. *Cost components* allow for cost breakdown with predetermined categories/buckets. The origin for each cost component needs to be defined, which is usually a cost element range group associated with that component.

Figure 7.19 shows the COST COMPONENT configuration setup (transaction OKTZ).

The menu path is as follows: TOOLS • CUSTOMIZING • IMG • SPRO EXECUTE PROJECT • CONTROLLING • PRODUCT COST CONTROLLING • PRODUCT COST PLANNING • BASIC SETTINGS FOR MATERIAL COSTING • DEFINE COST COMPONENT STRUCTURE.

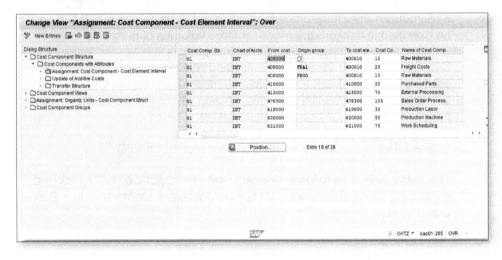

Figure 7.19: OKTZ — Cost component setup

Figure 7.20 shows results of the COST COMPONENT view of DISPLAY MATERIAL COST ESTIMATE WITH QUANTITY STRUCTURE (transaction CK13N).

CComp	Name of Cost Comp.	Σ	Overall Σ	Fixed Σ	Variable	Crcy
10	Raw Materials		3,000.00		3,000.00	USD
20	Purchased Parts					USD
25	Freight Costs					USD
30	Production Labor					USD
40	Production Setup					USD
50	Production Machine		1,250.00	1,100.00	150.00	USD
60	Production Burn-In					USD
70	External Processing					USD
75	Work Scheduling					USD
80	Material Overhead					USD
90	Equipment Internal					USD
95	Equipment External					USD
120	Other Costs		340.00	40.00	300.00	USD
200	Process "Production"					USD
210	Process"Procurement"					USD
		■	**4,590.00** ■	**1,140.00** ■	**3,450.00**	**USD**

Cost Components for Material FG-1001 Plant CHC1

Figure 7.20: CK13N— Cost estimate cost component view

7.9   Reporting in product cost planning

Alex made note of product costing related important transactions in a table (see Figure 7.21) for his reference.

Master Data Object	Create	Change	Display	Others
Material Master	MM01	MM02	MM03	MM60 - Material List
Bill of Material	CS01	CS02	CS03	CS11 - Explode BOM
				CS15 - Where-used list
				CS20 - Mass change
Work Center	CR01	CR02	CR03	CR05 - Work Center List
				CR06 - Cost Center Assignment
Routing	CA01	CA02	CA03	CA85 - Replace Work Center
Resource	CRC1	CRC2	CRC3	CA81 - Where-used list
Master Recipe	C201	C202	C203	C251 - Recipe List
Production Version	C223			

Master Data Objects and their transaction codes

Cost Estimate	Transaction
Create Cost Estimate	CK11N
Display Cost Estimate	CK13N
Mark / Release Costing	CK24
Costing Run	CK40N

Costing reports	Transaction
List of Existing Material Cost Estimates	S_P99_41000111
Analyze Costing Runs	S_ALR_87099930
Analyze / Compare Costing Runs	S_ALR_87099931
Variances Between Costing Runs	S_ALR_87099932

Select Configuration	Transaction
Costing Variant	OKKN
Valuation Variant	OKK4
Costing Sheet	KZS2
Cost Components	OKTZ

Other costing options	Transaction
Additive Costs	CK74
Mixed Costing- Procurement Alternatives	CK91N
Mixing Ratios	CK94

Figure 7.21: Product costing transaction codes

8 Production planning and controlling: Where everything in the plant is clearly visible

> "Manufacturing is more than just putting parts together.
> It's coming up with ideas, testing principles, and
> perfecting the engineering, as well as final assembly."
> — James Dyson

Because of the tightly integrated nature of the SAP Enterprise Resource Planning (ERP) system, it is important that the controller is aware of everything that happens in the production planning area. Because a lot of what production planning does (or at times, does not do) affects controlling, good insight into shop floor transactions is key to understanding the impact on the plant's financial performance.

Before production planning can begin creating transactions, there are prerequisites on the controlling side that must be set up.

▶ Standard costs must exist for the material and its components.

▶ Activity prices must exist for the activities used in routing / recipe.

Regular production planning and shop floor execution activities can begin once these prerequisites are met.

8.1 Create a process order

MRP controllers usually use an MRP run to create orders. Orders can be created directly from transaction COR1. Various steps such as scheduling, material availability check, order release, and preliminary costing are performed.

The menu path is as follows: LOGISTICS • PRODUCTION - PROCESS • PROCESS ORDER • PROCESS ORDER • CREATE • WITH MATERIAL.

Production orders use transaction CO01. There are differences between production orders and process orders, but the data flow and behind-the-scenes accounting and controlling impact is similar.

The menu path is as follows: LOGISTICS • PRODUCTION • SHOP FLOOR CONTROL • ORDER • CREATE • WITH MATERIAL.

A process order is created for a material and plant combination for a given order type. The order type determines what kind of production can be carried out (for example, PI01 for a finished material, PI11 for a semi-finished material, PI99 for R&D trials, and PI98 for rework orders, etc.) and what settlement rule will be adopted for the order.

See Figure 8.1 for an example of the CREATE PROCESS ORDER: INITIAL SCREEN.

Create Process Order: Initial Screen

Material Number	FG-1001
Production Plant	CHC1
Planning Plant	
Process Order Type	PI01
Process Order	

Copy from
Process Order	

| COR1 | sap01-205 | OVR |

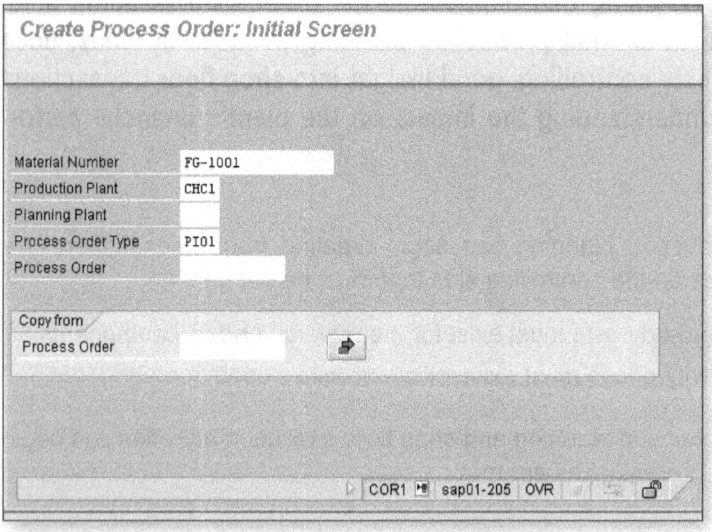

Figure 8.1: COR1 — Create process order initial screen

Components are pulled from the bill of materials and operations are pulled from the master recipe. Depending on the design, shop floor personnel can make modifications in process orders. However, as far as possible, it is best practice to keep the master data accurate and up to date in order to prevent problems during shop floor execution. After the material, plant, and order type are entered, the next screen shows the process order header screen (see Figure 8.2).

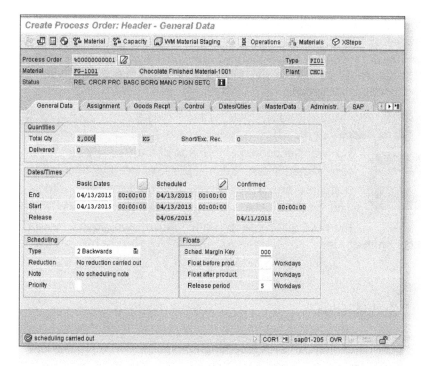

Figure 8.2: COR1 — Create process order

A settlement rule is created for the process order, depending on the order type used. Figure 8.3 shows settlement of order to material. This means that any variances that occur on this process order will be settled (transferred) to the material.

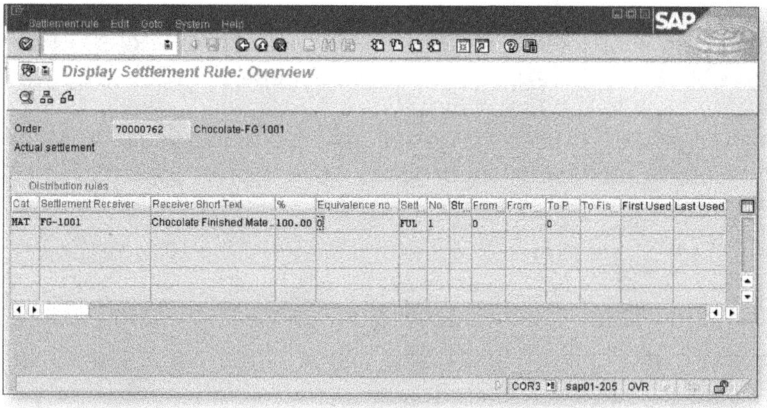

Figure 8.3: COR3 — Process order settlement rule

The settlement rule determines how the variances on the order will be disposed of. The most widely used settlement rule is to settle to the material (used for regular production), other options include settlement to cost center (used for R&D trials), GL account, and project/ WBS element (used for capital projects).

No financial postings at order creation stage

 No financial postings are made at the time of order creation. Material reservations are created, but until these materials are issued, there are no financial postings. The order will start receiving actual costs when one or more of goods issue, confirmation, and goods receipt occur on the order.

8.2 Goods issue

Shop floor personnel can start recording transactions on a process order once the MRP controller has released the order. An order gets the first set of actual costs when issue of goods (components) occurs.

Goods issue is a posting in the system that records the issuance of inventory into a CO object (process order, internal order, or cost center). Goods issue is usually performed using transaction MB1A, or by way of transactions, such as MIGO, MIGO_GI (see Figure 8.4).

The menu path is as follows: LOGISTICS • PRODUCTION - PROCESS • ENVIRONMENT • MATERIAL MOVEMENT • WITHDRAW MATERIAL.

Movement type 261 is used for goods issue on production/process orders. A reversal (or cancellation) of goods issue to order uses movement type 262.

Movement types are fundamental to the materials management module and along with valuation class, drive the financial postings that occur for a given transaction.

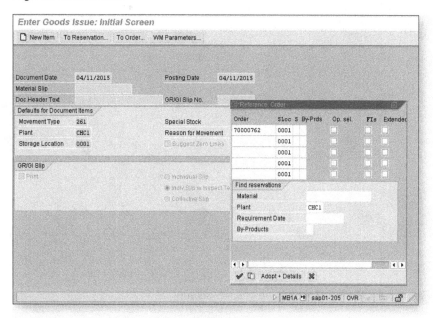

Figure 8.4: MB1A — Goods issue initial screen

One can enter the actual quantity of raw material spent on the order, if available (see Figure 8.5). *Direct issue* occurs when the actual quantity is entered. *Backflushing* occurs when the default quantity proposed by the bill of material is consumed on the order. This would imply that there will be no variance on the order, given that the actual quantity is same as standard quantity. To backflush or not, is therefore a very critical design decision that needs to be carefully evaluated at the time of project implementation phase. Most organizations try to bring a balance between accuracy of data capture (achieved by direct issue) and efficiency of data capture (achieved by backflushing).

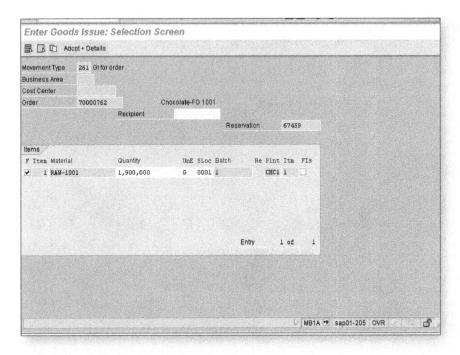

Figure 8.5: MB1A — Goods issue quantity screen

The system provides a material document number once the goods issue transaction is saved (see Figure 8.6). One can review the material, quantity consumed, plant, storage location, batch number, order, movement type, etc. from this material document.

The menu path is as follows: LOGISTICS • MATERIALS MANAGEMENT • INVENTORY MANAGEMENT • MATERIAL DOCUMENT • DISPLAY.

This material document will generally have accounting documents created in the background, based on the system setup for movement type, valuation class, and type of transaction (see Figure 8.7). Valuation class, along with movement type, influences a lot of these financial postings.

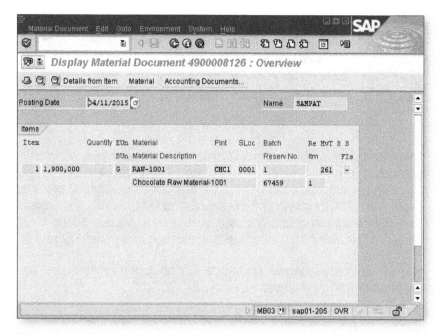

Figure 8.6: MB1A — Goods issue material document

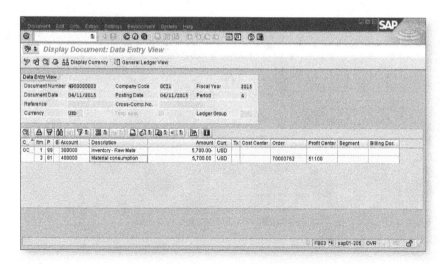

Figure 8.7: MB1A — Goods issue accounting document

Accounting impact at goods issue

The system credits the INVENTORY-RAW MATERIAL GL account, and debits the MATERIAL CONSUMPTION GL account and process order, at the time of goods issue.

Transactions performed on process orders are immediately reflected in the PROCESS ORDER COST ANALYSIS screen. The process order display menu path (transaction code COR3 • GOTO • COSTS • ANALYSIS) provides a good view of costs posted on the process order including plan versus actual comparison and target versus actual comparison. Goods issue postings are recorded on the debit side of process order (see Figure 8.8).

The menu path is as follows: LOGISTICS • PRODUCTION - PROCESS • PROCESS ORDER • PROCESS ORDER • DISPLAY.

Transaction	Origin	Origin (Text)	Σ Total plan quantity	Σ	Total target qty	Σ	Total Actual Qty	Σ	Total plan costs	Σ	Total target costs	Σ	Total actual costs	Target/actual var	Currency
Goods Issues	CHC1/RAW-1001	Chocolate Raw Material-1001	2,000.000		0		1,900.000		6,000.00		0.00		5,700.00	5,700.00	USD
Goods Issues			2,000.000	•	0	•	1,900.000	•	6,000.00	•	0.00	•	5,700.00		USD
Confirmations	C51100/LABOR	Choctwn-Choclat-M1 / Labor Hours	20.00		0.00		0.00		736.00		0.00		0.00	0.00	USD
	C51100/MCHRS	Choctwn-Choclat-M1 / Machine Hours	30.00		0.00		0.00		2,220.00		0.00		0.00	0.00	USD
Confirmations			50.00	•	0.00	•	0.00	•	2,956.00	•	0.00	•	0.00		USD
Goods Receipt	CHC1/FG-1001	Chocolate Finished Material-1001	2,000-		0		0		9,180.00-		0.00		0.00	0.00	USD
Goods Receipt			2,000-	•	0	•	0	•	9,180.00-	•	0.00	•	0.00		USD
			2,000.000	••	0	••	1,900.000	••	224.00-	••	0.00	••	5,700.00		USD
			50.00		0.00		0.00								
			2,000-		0		0								

Figure 8.8: COR3 — Process order costs after goods issue

8.3 Confirmation

A *confirmation* is a document that records the work that has be done for an operation. *Operations* are production steps that can have materials or activities assigned to them.

Once the goods are issued to the order, it is now time to record the number of hours to manufacture the product on that order.

A confirmation is usually performed using transaction COR6N (see Figure 8.9), or using transactions CORK or KB21N.

The menu path is as follows: LOGISTICS • PRODUCTION - PROCESS • CONFIRMATION • ENTER FOR PHASE • TIME TICKET.

The confirmation transaction brings over quantities for activities from the process order. The COR6N screen defaults are 1,800 minutes (30 hours) for machine and 1,200 minutes (20 hours) for labor. However, this was manually updated to the actual time spent of 1,900 minutes (31.667 hours) for machine and 1,300 minutes (21.667 hours) for labor.

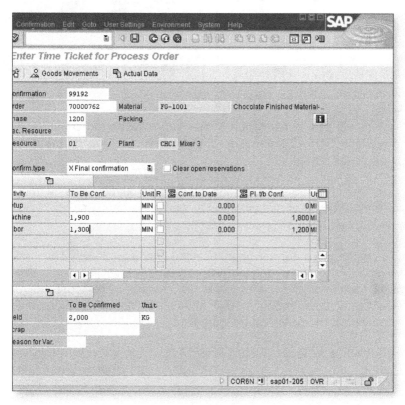

Figure 8.9: COR6N — Process order confirmation

The confirmation records the activity quantity on the order (see Figure 8.10). One can enter the actual activity spent on the order, if available.

Such as with goods issue, direct issue, or a backflushing decision is necessary for the confirmation step.

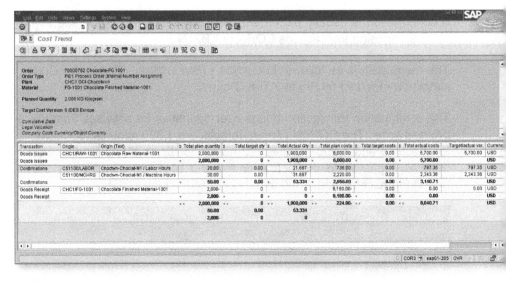

Figure 8.10: COR3 — Process order costs after confirmation

The cost impact of a confirmation transaction is displayed concurrently on the process order. Confirmation postings are recorded on the debit side of a process order.

As you will see in Figure 8.9, even though the plan quantity was 20 hours of labor and 30 hours of machine hours, we ended up spending 21.667 hours on labor and 31.667 hours on machine hours.

The cost center and order are both impacted during an activity confirmation on order. An order is debited with the activity quantity (and value) confirmed, whereas the cost center is credited. The cost center plan/actual comparison report S_ALR_87013611 reflects this information immediately on confirmation (see Figure 8.11).

The menu path is as follows: ACCOUNTING • CONTROLLING • COST CENTER ACCOUNTING • INFORMATION SYSTEM • PLAN/ACTUAL COMPARISONS • COST CENTERS: ACTUAL/PLAN/VARIANCE.

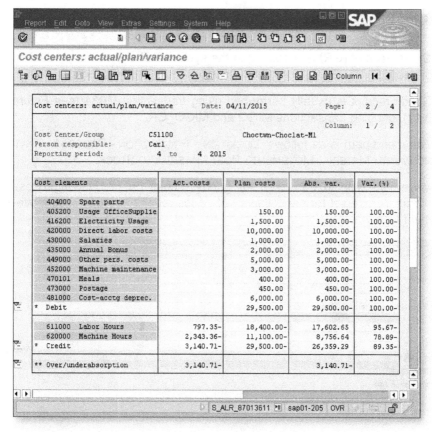

Figure 8.11: S_ALR_87013611 — Cost center report after confirmation

Accounting impact on confirmation

The system credits the activity type secondary cost element and cost center and debits the activity type secondary cost element and process order at the time of activity confirmation.

8.4 Goods receipt

Goods receipt (GR) is a posting in the system that shows the production of goods.

Goods receipt is usually performed using transaction MB31 (see Figure 8.12), or using transactions MIGO and MIGO_GR.

The menu path is as follows: LOGISTICS • PRODUCTION - PROCESS • ENVIRONMENT • MATERIAL MOVEMENT • POST MATERIAL TO STOCK.

Movement type 101 is used for goods receipt on production/process orders. A reversal (or cancellation) of goods receipt to order uses movement type 102.

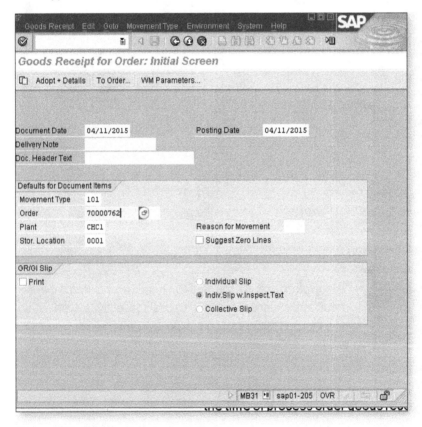

Figure 8.12: MB31 — Goods receipt initial screen

In the example in Figure 8.13, the actual production happened to be 2,100 KG, even though there was a plan to make 2,000 KG on the process order. The additional quantity of 100 KG is often referred to as *over delivery*. Whereas plan costs for the order will be calculated based on the plan quantity of 2,000 KG, the target costs for the order will be calculated based on the actual quantity of 2,100 KG.

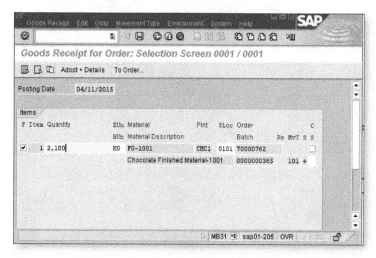

Figure 8.13: MB31 — Goods receipt quantity screen

Like in the case of goods issue, the goods receipt transaction also creates a material document (see Figure 8.14). One can review the material, quantity produced, plant, storage location, batch number, order, movement type, etc. from the material document.

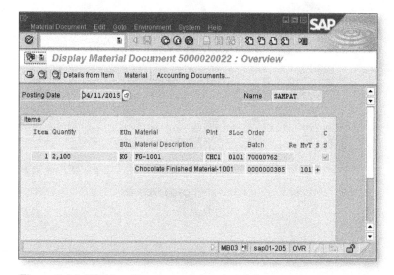

Figure 8.14: MB31 — Goods receipt material document

Similarly, this material document will have accounting documents created in the background, based on the system setup for movement type, valuation class, and type of transaction (see Figure 8.15).

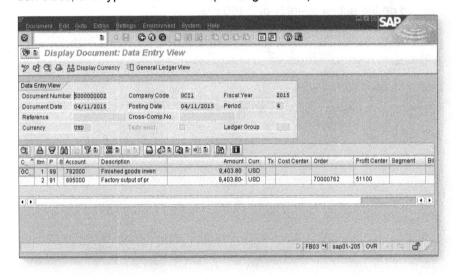

Figure 8.15: MB31 — Goods receipt accounting document

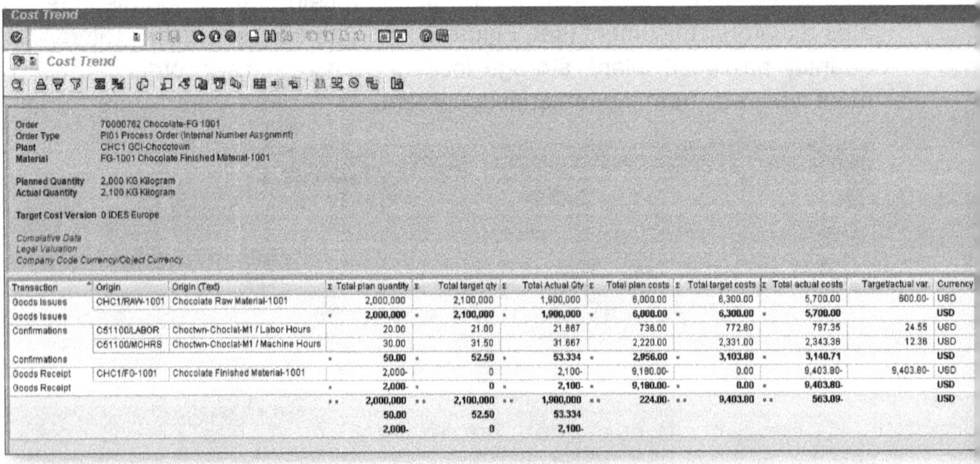

Figure 8.16: COR3 — Process order costs after goods receipt

The goods receipt transaction records the production on a process order by posting the quantity and value on the credit side on the process order (see Figure 8.16). Additionally, target quantity and cost are updated and adjusted for the actual production quantity.

Accounting impact at goods receipt

 The system credits the factory output production (also known as production value) GL account and process order, and debits the inventory GL account at the time of process order goods receipt.

Alex recapped list of transactions for production planning and controlling (see Table 8.1).

Transaction code	Description
COR1	Create process order
COR2	Change process order
COR3	Display process order
COR3 • Goto • Costs • Analysis	Display process order costs
CO01	Create production order
MB1A	Enter goods issue
MB03	Material document display
FB03	Accounting document display
COR6N	Enter confirmation
MB31	Enter goods receipt
MIGO	Enter goods movement
MIGO_GI	Enter goods issue
MIGO_GR	Enter goods receipt

Table 8.1: Transactions codes for production planning and controlling

9 Month-end close: Your organization's status report

> *"Month end is approaching — keep calm and carry on accounting."*
> —Anonymous

"Month-end is approaching," Bob said to Alex. "You should know the steps that we perform in finance during this time. We have been doing this every month for several years now. The steps include process order WIP, variance, settlement, and analysis."

Alex could relate—at FLW, materials, production, and finance performed coordinated tasks during the last few days of the month being closed, and the activities continued into the first few days of the new month.

9.1 Cycle count and distribution of usage variances

The physical inventory count (also known as cycle count) is performed by materials and shop floor personnel. Depending on whether there was a net increase or net decrease in the physical inventory versus system inventory, a gain or loss is posted on the income statement.

Whereas cycle count is more of a shop floor and/or warehouse activity, there are finance and internal control implications that result from these transactions. Hence, finance should be aware of the process. Additionally, some organizations want to spread cycle count differences to production/process orders that ran in the recent past. This process is supported by the *distribution of usage variances* (DUV) functionality found in SAP software.

Process orders are settled at month end. Depending on their status, some orders may be incomplete and need to be carried forward to the next month. Completed orders qualify for variance calculation, whereas incomplete orders are treated as work-in-process.

9.2   Process order status

The system assigns various statuses to an order in the course of the order's lifecycle. For example, order status CRTD (created) is set at the time of order creation, REL (released) is set at the time of release, PDLV (partially delivered) at the time of partial delivery, DLV (delivered) at the time of final delivery, and TECO (technically complete) at the time of technical completion. Order status determines what type of business transactions can be allowed and it therefore plays an important role in the order lifecycle.

Status for an order can be reviewed from COR3 by clicking the "Status" button ⓘ. Figure 9.1 shows various statuses set for an example order.

Statuses that are important from a finance perspective include:

- ▶ REL — released. This status is set when an order is released. The status allows all actual and committed values to be posted to the order.

- ▶ PRC — pre-costed. Indicates that a plan cost estimate exists for an order.

- ▶ PDLV — partially delivered. This status is set during goods receipt if only part of the planned quantity has been delivered.

- ▶ DLV — delivered. This status is set if either the planned quantity of an object has been delivered, or if the delivery completed indicator has been set during goods receipt.

- ▶ TECO — technical completion. This means ending a production order from a logistical viewpoint. This function is typically used if the execution of an order has to be stopped prematurely, or if the order could not be executed in the required manner and open requirements for the order (reservations, capacities, etc.) should be deleted.

- ▶ VCAL — variances calculated. This status is set by the system when you have calculated variances for an order.

- ▶ RESA — results analysis carried out. This status is set by the system when you have performed a WIP calculation for an order.

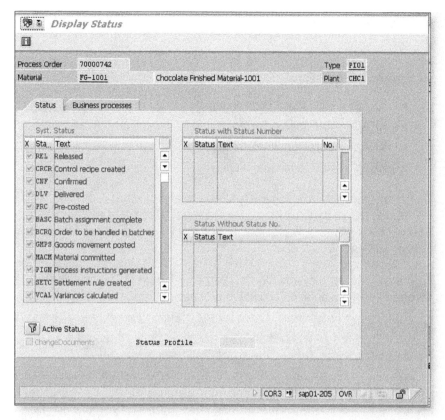

Figure 9.1: COR3 — Order status display

Completed versus incomplete orders

Completed orders: Completed orders are those orders for which the system status is either DLV (delivered) or TECO (technically completed) or both.

Incomplete (or WIP) orders: WIP orders are those orders that have costs posted against them and the system status is neither DLV (delivered), nor TECO (technically complete).

9.3 Work-in-progress

Incomplete orders (also referred to as WIP orders) are processed using the following transactions:

- ► KKAO — WIP mass processing
- ► KKAQ — WIP mass display
- ► KKAX — WIP individual processing
- ► KKAY — WIP individual display

The menu path is as follows: CONTROLLING • PRODUCT COST CONTROLLING • COST OBJECT CONTROLLING • PRODUCT COST BY ORDER • PERIOD-END CLOSING • SINGLE FUNCTIONS • WORK IN PROCESS • COLLECTIVE PROCESSING • KKAO – CALCULATE.

Figure 9.2 shows the selection screen and Figure 9.3 shows the result screen for WIP calculation collective processing transaction KKAO.

SAP's WIP process does not mean that we are talking about semi-finished materials!

 Many organizations refer to semi-finished materials as "WIP materials" and may confuse SAP's WIP process with semi-finished materials, but these are two different things. SAP's WIP (work-in-process) calculation is a process to carry forward the balance for an incomplete order. Whereas "WIP materials" are sometimes known as an alternate term for semi-finished materials.

WIP calculation does not post any financial entries!

 WIP calculation transaction does not post any entries, it merely calculates the amount to be carried over as WIP. A WIP entry is posted when settlement transaction is executed.

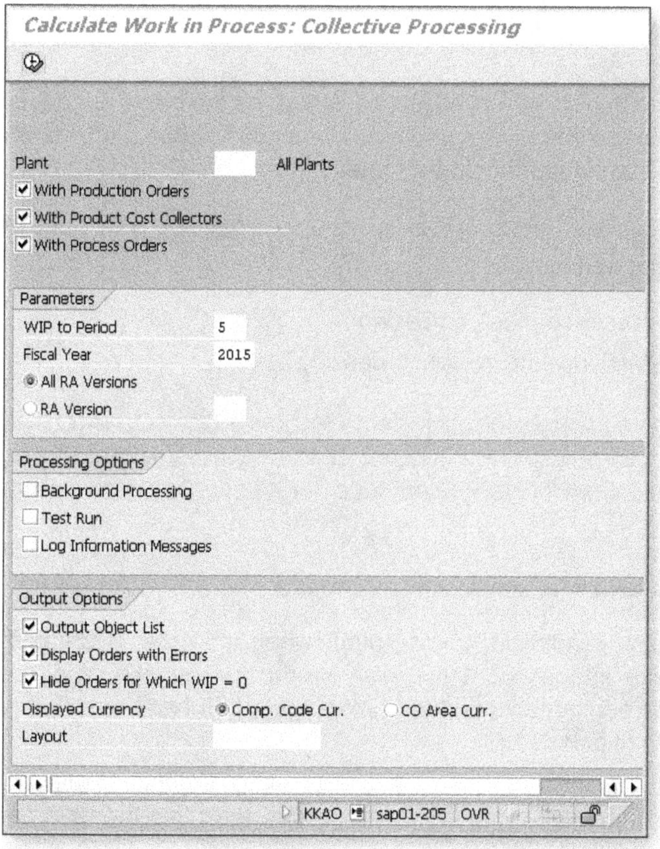

Figure 9.2: KKAO — WIP collective processing selection screen

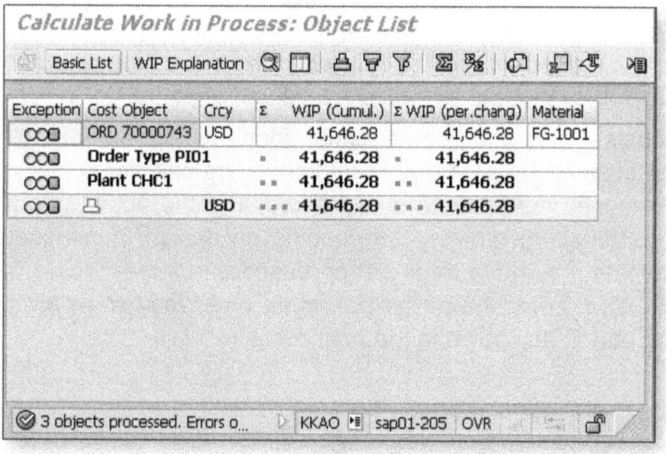

Figure 9.3: KKAO — WIP collective processing result screen

137

9.4 Variance calculation

Completed orders qualify for variance calculation. As the name suggests, the system calculates target versus actual variances. Targets are determined based on the standard cost estimate.

Completed orders (with status or either DLV or TECO) are processed using the following transactions:

- ▶ KKS1 — Variance mass processing
- ▶ KKS2 — Variance individual processing

The menu path is as follows CONTROLLING • PRODUCT COST CONTROLLING • COST OBJECT CONTROLLING • PRODUCT COST BY ORDER • PERIOD-END CLOSING • SINGLE FUNCTIONS • VARIANCES • KKS1 - COLLECTIVE PROCESSING.

At this point, we have seen several types of costs.

- ▶ Plan costs — Collected on the order when the order is created. They take into account the plan production quantity and are based on components pulled from usage 1 BOM and modified in the order (if permitted).

- ▶ Actual costs — Recorded when one or more of goods issue, activity confirmation, or goods receipt occur. Note that the term *actual costs* comes with a caveat. Components quantity may be based on actual cost; material price is based on standard cost of the components and is not actual cost. Similarly, the activity quantities may be based on actual, but the price is based on the planned price of activities. It is only when the orders are revalued with actual price that the activities are valued at actual.

- ▶ Target costs — Recorded when actual goods receipt and/or variance calculation is carried out. Target costs are calculated based on the released cost estimate in proportion of the actual goods receipt (production) quantity. Depending on design, a released cost estimate may have been set up based on usage 1 BOM or usage 6 BOM. Thus, the target cost in an order may show a different number than shown in the plan costs.

Figure 9.4 shows the selection screen and Figure 9.5 shows the result screen for variance calculation collective processing transaction KKS1.

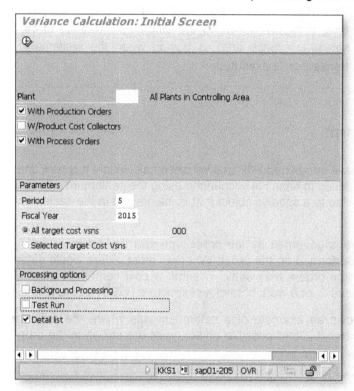

Figure 9.4: KKS1 — Variance calculation selection screen

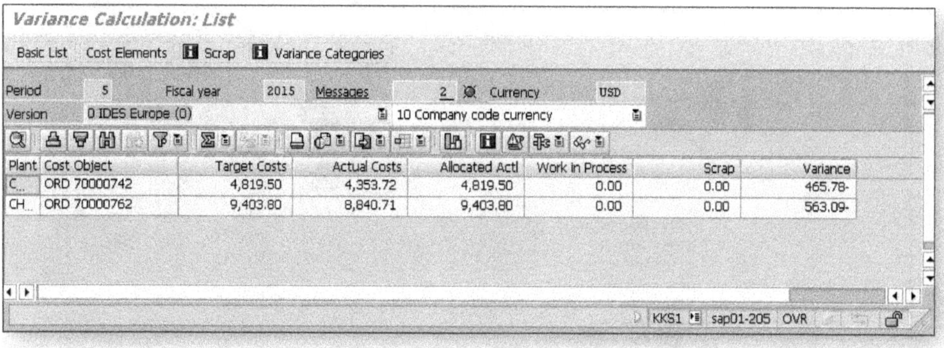

Figure 9.5: KKS1 — Variance calculation result screen

139

Variance calculation does not post any financial entries!

Variance calculation transaction does not post any entries, it merely calculates the amount of variance to be settled. Variance entry is posted when the settlement transaction is executed.

9.5 Settlement

Now that we have completed WIP and variance calculation, it is now time to post these values to financial accounting using the settlement process. An order is settled to a specific object that is maintained in the settlement rule.

Settlement rule is governed by the order type and the nature of activity/production performed on the order. Whereas most orders would settle to material, some orders may settle to either a cost center, an internal order, a GL account, or a work breakdown structure (WBS) element.

Figure 9.6 shows an example of a settlement rule where the order is settled to a material. Other possible object types are shown in the drop-down menu.

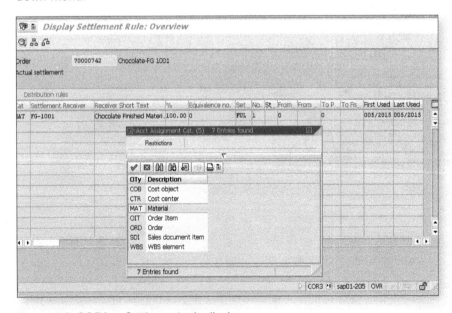

Figure 9.6: COR3— Settlement rule display

Settlement is performed using the following transactions:

► CO88 — Settlement mass processing.

► KO88 — Settlement individual processing.

The menu path is as follows CONTROLLING • PRODUCT COST CONTROLLING • COST OBJECT CONTROLLING • PRODUCT COST BY ORDER • PERIOD-END CLOSING • SINGLE FUNCTIONS • SETTLEMENT • CO88 - COLLECTIVE PROCESSING.

Figure 9.7 shows the selection screen.

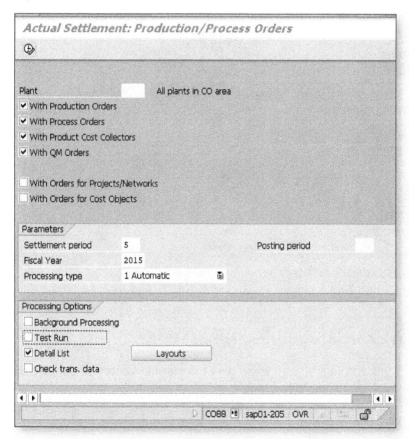

Figure 9.7: CO88 — Settlement selection screen

Figure 9.8 shows the results screen for settlement posting collective processing transaction CO88.

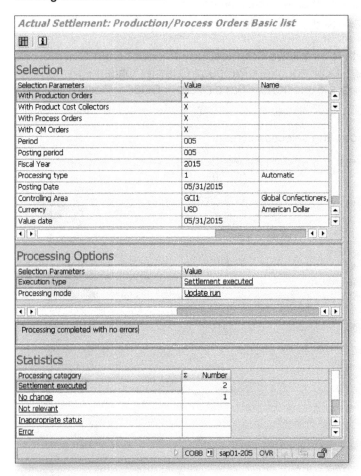

Figure 9.8: CO88 — Settlement result screen

Figure 9.9 and Figure 9.10 show an FI document posted at the time of settlement for a completed order.

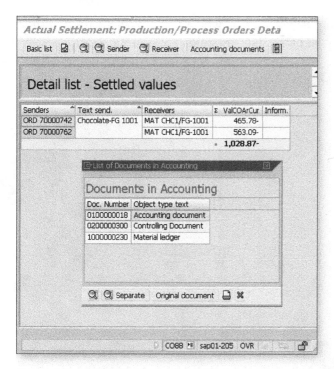

Figure 9.9: CO88 — Settlement detail list

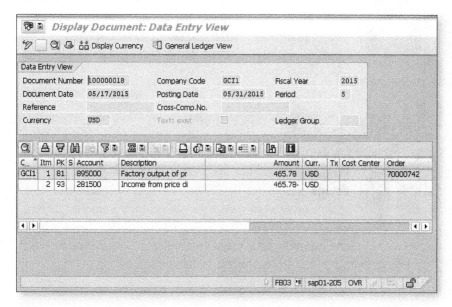

Figure 9.10: CO88 — Settlement FI document completed order

Figure 9.11 shows COR3 costs display and a new record for SETTLEMENT in the order. The order balance is now zero.

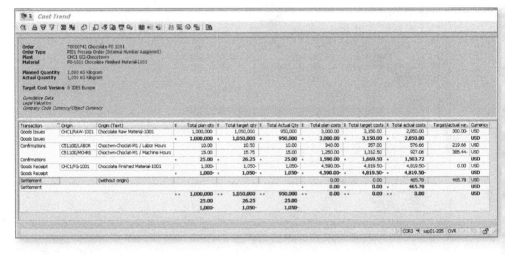

Figure 9.11: COR3 — Costs after settlement

Financial entry at WIP

WIP entry at settlement posts to the P&L and balance sheet accounts configured for carrying forward balances to the next month. Cost display in COR3 is not affected (that is, the WIP amount is not reflected as a separate line in the COR3 cost display).

Do not create a production variance and WIP P&L GL account as a cost element!

Production variance and work in process P&L GL accounts should not be created as cost elements due to a technical requirement for WIP and variances. These values are being transferred from CO to FI and if they are created as a cost element, then FI will try to post them again in CO, thereby leading to duplication!

Figure 9.12 displays an accounting document posted for a WIP order.

C...	Itm	PK	S	Account	Description	Amount	Curr.	Assignment	Tx
GCI1	1	50		893000	Inventory in process	41,646.28-	USD	70000743	
	2	40		793000	WIP	41,646.28	USD	70000743	

Figure 9.12: CO88 — Settlement FI document WIP order

WIP entry is reversed when an order is completed

WIP values will automatically be reversed during the subsequent period's settlement once the orders are set to TECO/DLV status. (Orders may not always be completed in the subsequent month, but may get completed after several months depending on the type of industry and the nature of product and/or production process).

An order usually has either WIP or variance posting in a particular month. An order may get both a WIP and a variance posting in the month in which an incomplete order is completed.

9.6 Reporting in cost object controlling

Apart from individual order display (COR3), there are certain mass order display transactions that can be very useful for performing queries on orders.

▶ COOIS — Production order information system.

▶ COOISPI — Process order information system.

▶ COID — Select object detail lists in PP-PI.

One of the reports that provides a financial summary of orders is the S_ALR_87013127 order balance report. Various columns are available; you can use the CHANGE LAYOUT option to select the right fields that match the requirement. Figure 9.13 is an example of some of the key fields that can be used in this report.

The menu path is as follows LOGISTICS • PRODUCTION - PROCESS • PROCESS ORDER • REPORTING • ORDER INFORMATION SYSTEM • PROCESS ORDER INFORMATION SYSTEM.

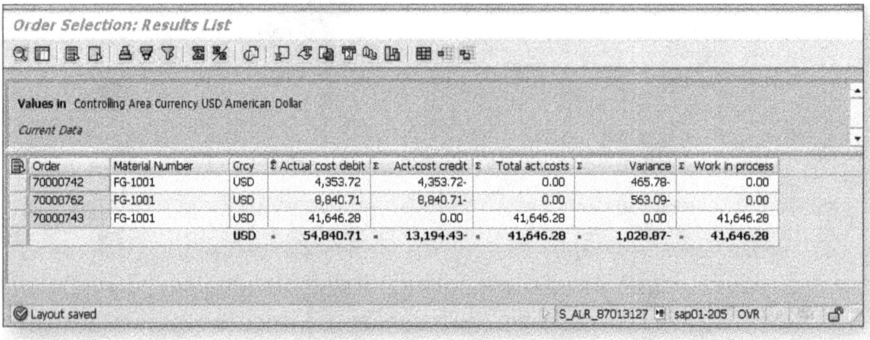

Order	Material Number	Crcy	Actual cost debit	Act.cost credit	Total act.costs	Variance	Work in process
70000742	FG-1001	USD	4,353.72	4,353.72-	0.00	465.78-	0.00
70000762	FG-1001	USD	8,840.71	8,840.71-	0.00	563.09-	0.00
70000743	FG-1001	USD	41,646.28	0.00	41,646.28	0.00	41,646.28
		USD	54,840.71	13,194.43-	41,646.28	1,028.87-	41,646.28

Figure 9.13: S ALR 87013127 — Order financial summary

Order summarization is another powerful reporting option available for orders. Data is collected on a periodic basis and can then be reviewed using transactions meant for reporting.

10 Actual costing and SAP Material Ledger: So this is where the actual costs reside...

"The cost of a thing is the amount of what I will call life which is required to be exchanged for it, immediately or in the long run."
— Henry David Thoreau

Knowing how much a product costs is essential to determine the accurate profitability of a product. Yet, most decisions are based on the standard cost of the product, given that many times it is not easy to get an accurate picture of the actual cost. Actual costing functionality provided by the material ledger component of SAP Controlling bridges this gap. It provides the ability to capture actual costs by tracking variances at the material (product) level. This chapter provides an overview of actual costing in SAP Material Ledger.

Bob walked into Alex's office one morning. "Hey Alex, can you help me look up the actual cost of cocoa butter for last month? Purchasing called me this morning and said that cocoa prices have been volatile for the last few months and will likely to go up again. As you know, this is one of the most widely used raw materials in our products and any change in its price is going to have a far-reaching impact on our product costs. We have been asked to provide information on our budget assumption versus what we actually paid for cocoa so far this year. It is possible that we may re-establish the standard for cocoa. Please identify the closing inventory quantities so that we can estimate the expected revaluation."

Alex knew where he could find the budget assumption — it was built in to the standard cost of the material and he could look it up in the MATERIAL MASTER COSTING 2 view. However, he was not sure where he could find the actual price. Alex turned to the user manual to see if he could find an answer. He found this information in the section on *Material Ledger*.

Material Ledger provides the functionality to derive actual costs and allow revaluation of inventory to actual costs," Alex read in the user manual. "This is exactly the information I was looking for," Alex said to himself and continued to read through the chapter with curiosity.

10.1 SAP Material Ledger overview

SAP Material Ledger inventory valuation includes the following broad steps:

- ▶ Collecting actual data during the month.
- ▶ Determining price: Single-level and multi-level prices are determined based on type of transactions performed.
- ▶ Calculating periodic unit price at the end of the month.

SAP Material Ledger collects *material movement* data throughout the month and keeps track of which materials were used for the production of which goods through production/process orders.

Single-level price determination calculates variances for each individual material; whereas *multi-level material price determination* calculates variances that flow to higher levels of the production process using a multi-level actual quantity structure.

Periodic unit price records the average actual cost for each material — whether procured or produced. Periodic unit price is calculated as a part of the period-end closing process for multi-level material determination.

Additionally, the system calculates an *actual cost component split.*

Actual cost component split

SAP Material Ledger calculates the breakdown of actual cost components of labor, material, overhead, sub-contracting, etc.

This information enables standard vs. actual or cross-period actual comparison at a low level of granularity.

SAP Material Ledger provides details for analysis, but may not always explain the reason for variances

 The SAP Material Ledger actual cost roll up is not necessarily a substitute for analysis of where and why cost differences occurred, but it provides a detailed level of information to efficiently drill down to postings that may have been responsible for a large abnormal/unexpected variance.

You can also use material ledger to record inventories in multiple currencies or valuations. This feature can be implemented independent from actual costing.

Without the material ledger, material can only be valued in one currency (company code currency). In the material ledger, inventory values can be carried in two additional currencies (total of 3 currencies). In other words, parallel valuation is possible using the material ledger.

Currency amounts are translated into foreign currencies at the prevailing exchange rate at the time of posting. This is achieved by updating all of the goods movements in up to three currencies/valuations in the material ledger.

The material ledger enables you to look at costs in three different currencies/structures:

▶ Legal view of the independent legal companies (company code view).

▶ Group view of the organization as whole (group currency view).

▶ Group valuation/profit center valuation used to support various reporting requirements, including the elimination of intercompany profits.

10.2 Collecting actual data during the month

The SAP Materials Management module (in combination with the FI module) tracks goods movements and their values at standard cost, while the SAP Material Ledger tracks goods movement values at standard and actual costs. In other words, SAP Material Ledger can be considered a second set of books where each material has a record of all goods movements for actual valuation.

All relevant inventory activity from SAP is posted to the material ledger.

▶ Inventory movements are reflected in the material ledger as goods movement transactions occur (for example, movement type 101 for goods receipt, 261 for goods issue, 551 for scrapping, 701 for cycle counts, 601 for sales, 201 for consumption at cost center, etc.).

▶ Price variances are reflected as they occur (for example, goods receipt records standard price versus purchase order price; invoice receipt records purchase order price versus invoice price).

▶ Production variances are reflected at the time of process/production order settlement.

▶ Revaluation differences are reflected at the time of standard changes (for example, at the beginning of the year or beginning of the month).

Figure 10.1 depicts transaction CKM3N (material price analysis). Material RAW-1001 had a BEGINNING INVENTORY of 9,050 grams, of which, 1,900 grams was consumed during the month as shown under the CONSUMPTION section, leaving an ENDING INVENTORY of 7,150 grams. Additionally, all of the transactions occurred at the STANDARD PRICE of $3.00 per 1,000 grams. However, there was one entry shown under DEBIT/CREDIT section for an amount of $9,050.00 that was driving the actual cost up to $4.00 per 1,000 grams as seen in the CUMULATIVE INVENTORY section of the report. Each goods movement transaction was reflected in this transaction. Users can navigate to the actual source document—for example an inventory movement transaction, price change, or settlement.

The menu path is as follows: ACCOUNTING • CONTROLLING • PRODUCT COST CONTROLLING • ACTUAL COSTING/MATERIAL LEDGER • MATERIAL LEDGER • CKM3 — MATERIAL PRICE ANALYSIS.

Figure 10.2 shows a finished material that had an opening inventory of 1,050 kilograms, 2,100 kilograms were produced during the month. Alex noticed a SINGLE-LEVEL DIFFERENCE on all of the rows including beginning inventory. Having single-level price differences in beginning inventory implied that the variances were being carried forward from the previous month.

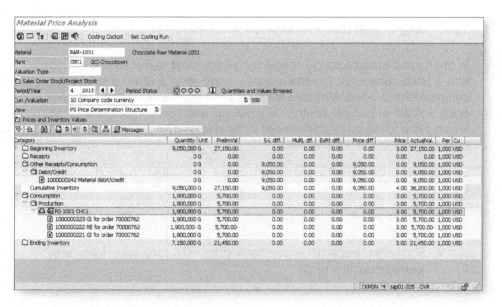

Figure 10.1: CKM3N — Price analysis of raw material prior to SAP Material Ledger close

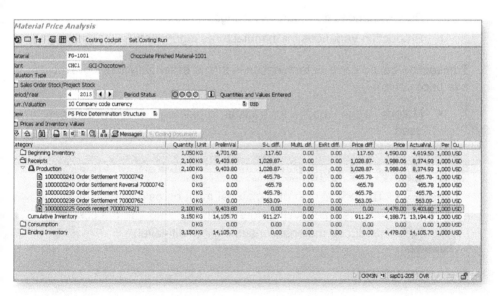

Figure 10.2: CKM3N — Price analysis finished material prior to SAP Material Ledger close

10.3 Single- and multi-level price determination

In the normal manufacturing operations where most materials are valued with a price control "S" (standard price), *single-level and multi-level price determination* is used. Materials such as plant maintenance that are generally valued with price control "V" (moving average price), there is no requirement to roll up the differences in the next level material, *transaction based price determination* is used.

Single-level price determination — prices are calculated for each individual material.

- ▶ Purchased material = standard price +/- price variance from purchases
- ▶ Produced material = standard price +/- variances from process/production order

Multi-level price determination — prices are calculated for the entire production stream (such as when rolling up all components or ingredients into a produced material).

- ▶ Price variances from purchased ingredients.
- ▶ Production variances for manufactured ingredients.

Transaction-based price determination — this is essentially moving average price control.

- ▶ Material ledger routine for transfer to higher-level material is not used.

Single-level price must be calculated before multi-level
The actual cost of a material must be calculated individually (single-level) before it can be rolled into the cost of produced material consuming it (multi-level).

10.4 Periodic unit price

Periodic unit price is nothing more than the average actual cost of a material in a given period. It is calculated based on the CUMULATIVE INVENTORY line in transaction CKM3N.

Periodic unit price = (standard cost of cumulative inventory +/- variances of cumulative inventory) / cumulative inventory.

As shown in Figure 10.3, a standard cost of $3.00 was used for goods issue during the month. A price variance of $9,050.00 for the given quantity of 9,050 grams (a variance of $1.00 per 1,000 grams) resulted in periodic unit price of the material of $4.00 per 1,000 grams. For the given consumption of 1,900 grams, the material ledger transferred the variance of $1,900 to the next level material. Additionally, a periodic unit price of $4.00 per 1,000 grams will be used to value ending inventory of 7,150 grams at $28,600.00.

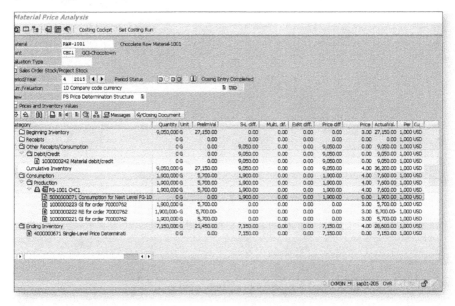

Figure 10.3: CKM3N — Price analysis raw material after SAP Material Ledger close

In Figure 10.4, note the material price analysis for finished material FG-1001. $1,900 was transferred from the lower level (RAW-1001) as a multi-level price difference. Additionally, process order settlement related variances of ($1,028.87) were recorded as a single-level price difference. At the cumulative inventory level, all of the variances were added up and divided by the cumulative inventory and periodic unit price was calculated as $4,791.88. This actual price was used to value closing inventory and transfer revaluation of consumption to the cost center.

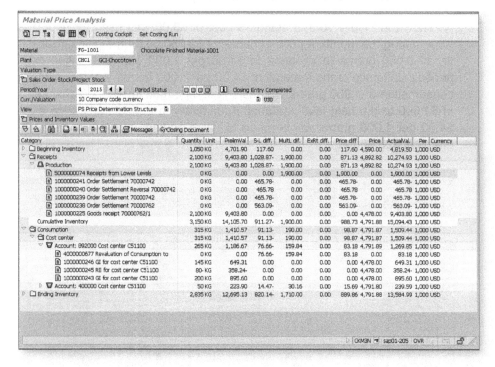

Figure 10.4: CKM3N — Price analysis finished material after SAP Material Ledger close

10.5   SAP Material Ledger closing cockpit

The SAP Material Ledger closing cockpit is run every month to perform actual costing using transaction code CKMLCP. The menu path is as follows: ACCOUNTING • CONTROLLING • PRODUCT COST CONTROLLING • ACTUAL COSTING/MATERIAL LEDGER • ACTUAL COSTING • CKMLCP — Edit Costing Run.

The first step is to create a costing run and assign relevant plants to the costing run. Figure 10.5 shows an example of actual costing run for 4/2015 with plant CHC1 assigned. There could be several plants attached to this costing run, depending on the material ledger footprint and business requirements.

Transparency across the value chain

 For SAP Material Ledger to transfer multi-level variances (and therefore actual cost) between plants, it is essential that the plants involved in interplant goods movement are closed in the same material ledger closing run.

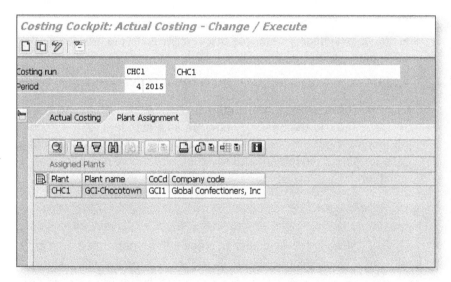

Figure 10.5: CKMLCP—ML closing cockpit plant selection

After selecting plant(s), the material ledger closing cockpit requires several steps. These steps should be performed in the same sequence as shown in Figure 10.6.

155

1. SELECTION — all materials for the given plants are selected.

2. SEQUENCE DETERMINATION — sequence of costing is established, starting with the lowest level material going all the way up to the highest level material and goods movement.

3. SINGLE-LEVEL PRICE DETERMINATION — prices are calculated for each individual material.

4. MULTI-LEVEL PRICE DETERMINATION — prices are calculated for the entire production stream.

5. REVALUATION OF CONSUMPTION — adjustment posting of actual costs at month end where all variances are transferred to the receiving object (which can be a material, or a cost center, internal order, GL account, etc. depending on where the original consumption occurred).

6. POST-CLOSING — all calculations performed in prior steps are posted during this step.

   ▶ Multi-level price differences are transferred to the next level.

   ▶ Revaluation of consumption is posted to cost objects.

   ▶ Inventory is revalued in FI for the period being closed.

7. MARK MATERIAL PRICES — this step is optional. An organization may decide not to use the periodic unit price as a standard for the upcoming month. If so, this step is skipped and the system uses standard price for goods movement and revalues at periodic unit price only at month end.

Actual costing calculation steps can be run multiple times

 Each of the calculation steps can be performed as many times as necessary. However, the post-closing step is performed only once in non-test mode. Reversal of the post-closing step is possible, but should be carried out only when absolutely necessary.

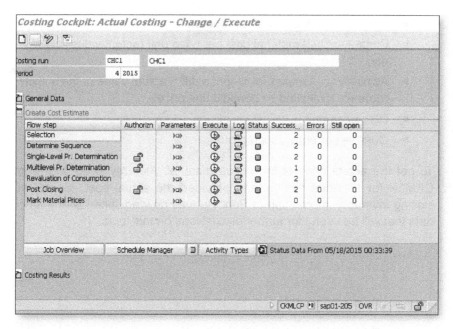

Figure 10.6: CKMLCP — SAP Material Ledger closing cockpit process steps

10.6 Reporting in SAP Material Ledger

Apart from CKM3N – material price analysis – there are a couple of other reports in SAP Material Ledger that are useful for analyzing data for several materials at a time. They include:

- ▶ S_P99_41000062 — Prices and inventory values
- ▶ S_ALR_87013181 — Material prices and inventory values over several periods

The columns in transaction CKM3N include:

- ▶ QUANTITY — quantity in the displayed unit of measure
- ▶ UNIT — base unit of measure
- ▶ PRELIMVAL — standard value (quantity multiplied by standard cost)
- ▶ S-L DIFF — single-level variance amount
- ▶ MULTL DIFF — multi-level variance amount
- ▶ EXRT DIFF — exchange rate difference

- ▶ PRICE DIFF — total variance amount
- ▶ PRICE — actual material cost per price unit (actual value / quantity)
- ▶ ACTUALVAL — prelimVal +/- price diff = actual value of the activity (quantity multiplied by periodic unit price)
- ▶ PER: price unit
- ▶ CURR — currency (local / group)

To get the actual price of the cocoa material, Alex reviewed data from CKM3N for previous months and provided the actual cost, as well as closing inventory information to Bob. He was now equipped with a lot of data that will be useful for further discussions on this topic.

11 Profitability analysis: Are we making any money at all?

"There was a small typing error in our Half-Year Results Statement. For 'profit' please read 'loss'."
—Ex – CFO.

Alex walked into the meeting room in the morning and saw his manager Bob, the plant controller at Chocotown. Bob had called an urgent meeting on short notice and wanted everyone to attend—Carl, the manufacturing manager; Dave, the inventory controller; and Erin, the finance IT support lead.

"Corporate is researching the profitability of the product line that we introduced last quarter," Bob said, "and they are telling me the product is not profitable."

"It can't be," Carl said. "We produced the material below the standard cost and all our variances have been favorable."

"And our inventory has been in control," said Dave.

"I understand what you are saying," said Bob, "but it is not only about cost. Moreover, the inventory levels do not affect profitability."

Dave was confused. "Well, I was told that I have to keep inventory in check so that our costs are lower."

Alex intervened. "That is correct, but the product profitability and inventory are not directly linked. There is a cost of carrying the inventory, but this cost is more related to locking working capital."

"Alex is right," Erin said. "Inventory is a balance sheet item, and it does not impact product profitability directly. If production cost is within the expected range, then it must have to do with the selling price."

Bob said, "Exactly! I have been telling corporate that marketing may not be selling the product at the budgeted price."

"Then I am I off the hook!" Carl had a sigh of relief.

"Not really," Bob said. "The analysis of the last three months' sales is in. They found that the product was sold at the budgeted price and the cost was within the range, but where we lost money was on the promotional discounts that we gave when we launched the product."

Carl said, "Oh boy! Then what do we do with the three out of the eight production lines that are scheduled to run this product for the next eight weeks? If you ask me to convert those back to earlier products, then we are going to need at least three days of down time. We cannot afford to do so when we are already running behind on shipments. If marketing has not factored in promotional cost, it is not our fault at the plant!"

"Erin, can you please provide your point of view?" Bob asked.

Alex valued Erin's opinion. After all, Erin had been in the role of finance IT support for a long time and she knew how the SAP system worked.

"Sure, Bob," Erin said. "I believe the data that corporate is looking at is from the profitability analysis module. It collects data on sales as well as costs, where we have sold how much product, in which market, in which channel, at what price, and at what discount, and so on. I believe something is going on with the new products that were introduced. Let's take a look at the system. I may not have a lot of business insight, but I can explain the data flow."

11.1 CO-PA overview

Profitability analysis (CO-PA) is a sub-module of SAP Controlling that enables an organization to evaluate market segments that can be classified according to product, customers, geographies, or any combination of these factors with respect to the organization's profit or *contribution margin* (often referred to as *gross margin*).

CO-PA provides management with information to support internal accounting and decision making from a market-oriented point of view.

Costing-based CO-PA uses characteristics and value fields to collect data. *Account-based CO-PA* creates reports using cost elements and characteristics, value fields are not used (essentially, cost elements are used to report the amount buckets).

A *profitability segment* is a collection of several characteristics.

Costing-based CO-PA calculates profits according to the cost-of-sales method of accounting, where the cost of sales is compared to revenue. The emphasis is on matching the cost with revenues, which allows for optimal analysis of the contribution margin.

Contribution margin is equal to sales revenues less variable costs. This amount offsets fixed expenses and produces an operating profit for the business.

Variable costs vary in proportion to sales levels. They can include direct material and labor costs, the variable part of manufacturing overhead costs, transportation costs, and sales commission expenses.

Fixed costs remain constant (for the most part) within the projected range of sales levels. They can include facilities costs, certain general and administrative costs, and interest and depreciation expenses.

All of the above terms are used for a *breakeven point* calculation to identify which segments are more profitable.

CO-PA and general ledger

CO-PA is not a general ledger system and cannot be used for external reporting. CO-PA uses data from several modules in SAP Controlling, including sales and distribution. CO-PA provides an analytical view of sales and operations for internal reporting and decision making.

11.2 Characteristics

Master data in CO-PA provides the fundamental data and content within the structures that are already determined. The master data is created when individual values are assigned to the characteristics and value fields. The combination of characteristics and values forms multidimensional profitability segments that are used as a basis for valuating operating results. The profitability segments represent the relevant market segments from the business point of view.

Characteristics created in the operating concern represent the criteria derived to provide a breakdown of operating results. SAP software contains many standard characteristics; however, if those characteristics do not satisfy reporting requirements then user-defined characteristics can also be created. Characteristics are the criteria in profitability analysis (CO-PA) according to which operating results are analyzed and differentiated sales and profit planning are performed.

Characteristics example

eg An organization wants to report on geography, country, region, customer channel, and product group (these will be defined as characteristics).

Within each characteristic, several possible values can be captured. For example, for geography: the Americas, Europe, Asia Pacific, and Africa. Or for country: the United States, Canada, Mexico, Brazil, and Argentina. Or region: Northeast, Mid-Atlantic, Midwest, Southwest, and Northwest. For customer channel: Direct Sale, Distributor, and Affiliate.

Characteristics are stored in field catalog and are maintained using transaction KEA5 as shown in Figure 11.1.

The menu path is as follows: TOOLS • CUSTOMIZING • IMG • SPRO EXECUTE PROJECT • CONTROLLING • PROFITABILITY ANALYSIS • STRUCTURES • DEFINE OPERATING CONCERN • MAINTAIN CHARACTERISTICS.

Characteristic derivation is the attempt to determine the characteristic values for all CO-PA characteristics in a given profitability relevant business transaction. The characteristic values that are transferred automatically are used to determine other logically dependent characteristics. To do so, the system can access information contained in the source document, as well as information existing outside of it.

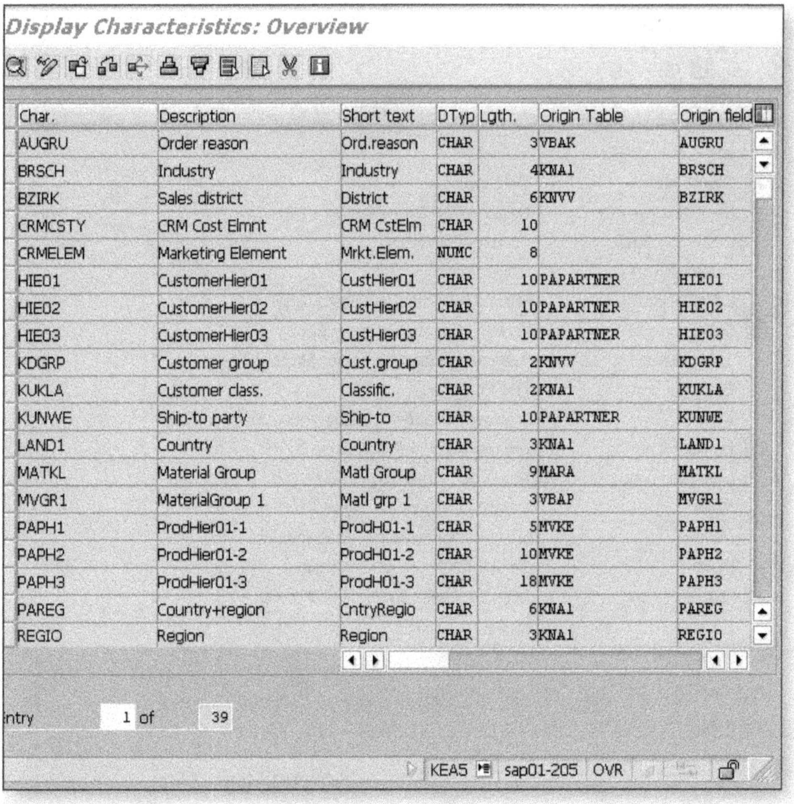

Display Characteristics: Overview

Char.	Description	Short text	DTyp	Lgth.	Origin Table	Origin field
AUGRU	Order reason	Ord.reason	CHAR	3	VBAK	AUGRU
BRSCH	Industry	Industry	CHAR	4	KNA1	BRSCH
BZIRK	Sales district	District	CHAR	6	KNVV	BZIRK
CRMCSTY	CRM Cost Elmnt	CRM CstElm	CHAR	10		
CRMELEM	Marketing Element	Mrkt.Elem.	NUMC	8		
HIE01	CustomerHier01	CustHier01	CHAR	10	PAPARTNER	HIE01
HIE02	CustomerHier02	CustHier02	CHAR	10	PAPARTNER	HIE02
HIE03	CustomerHier03	CustHier03	CHAR	10	PAPARTNER	HIE03
KDGRP	Customer group	Cust.group	CHAR	2	KNVV	KDGRP
KUKLA	Customer class.	Classific.	CHAR	2	KNA1	KUKLA
KUNWE	Ship-to party	Ship-to	CHAR	10	PAPARTNER	KUNWE
LAND1	Country	Country	CHAR	3	KNA1	LAND1
MATKL	Material Group	Matl Group	CHAR	9	MARA	MATKL
MVGR1	MaterialGroup 1	Matl grp 1	CHAR	3	VBAP	MVGR1
PAPH1	ProdHier01-1	ProdH01-1	CHAR	5	MVKE	PAPH1
PAPH2	ProdHier01-2	ProdH01-2	CHAR	10	MVKE	PAPH2
PAPH3	ProdHier01-3	ProdH01-3	CHAR	18	MVKE	PAPH3
PAREG	Country+region	CntryRegio	CHAR	6	KNA1	PAREG
REGIO	Region	Region	CHAR	3	KNA1	REGIO

ntry   1 of   39

KEA5   sap01-205   OVR

Figure 11.1: KEA5— Characteristics maintenance

Figure 11.2 displays transaction KEDR where characteristic derivation strategy is maintained.

The menu path is as follows: TOOLS • CUSTOMIZING • IMG • SPRO EXECUTE PROJECT • CONTROLLING • PROFITABILITY ANALYSIS • STRUCTURES • MASTER DATA • DEFINE CHARACTERISTIC DERIVATION.

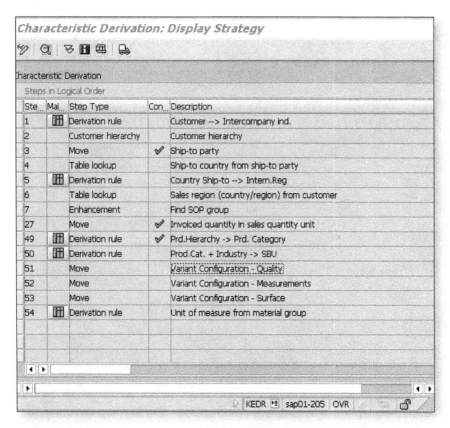

Figure 11.2: KEDR — Characteristic derivation strategy

Figure 11.3 displays the rule for the derivation of a product category based on product hierarchy.

Profitability segment is a cost object within profitability analysis where costs and revenues are assigned. A profitability segment is defined by a combination of characteristic values. The combination of characteristic values forms multidimensional profitability segments that are used as a basis for valuating operating results. The profitability segments represent the relevant market segments from the business point of view.

Figure 11.3: KEDR — Characteristic rule value

Profitability segment example

1. Americas + United States + Midwest + Distributor

2. Europe + Germany + Bavaria + Affiliate

3. Asia Pacific + Australia + New South Wales + Direct Sale

4. Africa + South Africa + Western Cape + Distributor

11.3 Value fields

In costing-based profitability analysis, *value fields* represent the highest level of detail at which quantities, revenues, sales deductions, and costs are analyzed. Mapping of revenues and costs into value fields can be freely defined at the time of system setup.

Value fields collect values such as revenues, sales deductions, costs, and quantities.

There are two types of value fields:

▶ Amount fields: Value fields that contain amounts in currencies. All amount fields in a single line item use the same currency.

▶ Quantity fields: Value fields that contain quantities.

Using value fields and mapping to cost elements

Value fields are only required in costing-based CO-PA (in account-based CO-PA, cost elements are used to report the amount buckets).

Mapping cost elements to a value field may result in several cost elements mapped to one value field, or in the case of settlement, one cost element broken down into several value fields. It is therefore important to thoroughly understand this mapping in order to efficiently reconcile CO-PA with FI.

Figure 11.4 displays transaction KEA6 where value fields are maintained for a given operating concern, with an indicator determining the type of update — amount or quantity.

The menu path is as follows: TOOLS • CUSTOMIZING • IMG • SPRO EXECUTE PROJECT • CONTROLLING • PROFITABILITY ANALYSIS • STRUCTURES • DEFINE OPERATING CONCERN • MAINTAIN VALUE FIELDS.

Value fields can be categorized according to how and when they are defined: predefined value fields (SAP delivered standard value fields) and user-defined value fields that start with "VV" (defined by that specific SAP installation).

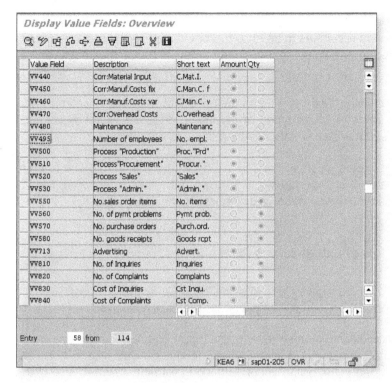

Figure 11.4: KEA6 — Value fields

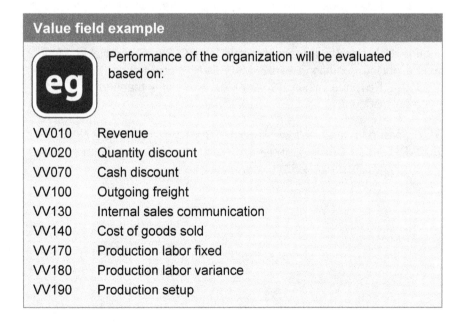

Value field example

Performance of the organization will be evaluated based on:

VV010	Revenue
VV020	Quantity discount
VV070	Cash discount
VV100	Outgoing freight
VV130	Internal sales communication
VV140	Cost of goods sold
VV170	Production labor fixed
VV180	Production labor variance
VV190	Production setup

Value fields need to be created according to the level of detail in which the operating result has to be shown. For example, each cost component is mapped to one value field to capture cost of goods manufactured details.

Generally, value fields are highly detailed with regards to sales performance figures (such as types of revenues, discounts, surcharges, etc.) and are summarized for other items relating to period costs.

Calculated items, such as net sales and contribution margin, are normally not created as separate value fields, but are calculated when reports are executed from the base values stored in the value fields.

11.4   Flow of actual values from billing

Posting data from sales and distribution (SD) normally constitutes the most important source of information for profitability analysis.

The SD module calculates revenues during billing using a pricing mechanism and then enters it in the billing document. Sales deductions are also recorded in the billing document, along with the standard cost of the goods sold.

Transfer of revenues from SD is configured in transaction KE4I where SD conditions are assigned to value fields.

Figure 11.5 depicts transaction KECM (CO-PA: Customizing Monitor) where pricing conditions PR02, VA00, VA01 are mapped to value field VV010 – Revenue; while K004, K020, K029 are mapped to VV040 — Material discount.

The menu path is as follows: TOOLS • CUSTOMIZING • IMG • SPRO EXECUTE PROJECT • CONTROLLING • PROFITABILITY ANALYSIS • TOOLS • ANALYSIS• CHECK CUSTOMIZING SETTINGS.

Value Field Analysis: Detail

Condition	Text - Condition	Value Fiel	Text - Value Field	+	A	S	Ac...	Accru...
PRO2	Price Increased	VV010	Revenue				ERL	
VA00	Variants						ERL	
VA01	Variants %						ERS	
ZA00	General variants						ERL	
KP00	Pallet Discount	VV020	Quantity discount				ERS	
K007	Customer Discount	VV030	Customer discount				ERS	
RA00	% Discount from Net						ERS	
K004	Material	VV040	Material discount				ERS	
K020	Price Group						ERS	
K029	Mat.Pricing Group						ERS	
K148	Product Hierarchy						ERS	
AMIZ	Minimum ValueSurchrg	VV060	Other rebates				ERS	
HA00	Percentage Discount						ERS	
HB00	Discount (Value)						ERS	
HI01	Hierarchy						ERS	
K005	Customer/Material						ERS	
K030	Customer/Mat.Pr.Grp						ERS	
K031	Price Grp/Mat.Pr.Grp						ERS	
KA00	Sales Promotion						ERS	
R100	100% discount						ERS	
ZVC0	Discount contract						ERS	
SKTO	Cash Discount	VV070	Cash discount		X			
SKTV	Cash Discount				X			

Figure 11.5: KECM — SD conditions mapped to value fields

When a sales invoice is generated, the system transfers all of the characteristics defined in profitability analysis and contained in the billing document, along with the customer and product numbers, from the document to the CO-PA line item. It also performs characteristic derivation for those fields for which derivation logic has been defined.

If the system recognizes an error (such as in characteristic derivation) while posting billing data to FI or CO-PA, it posts the billing document in SD anyway, but updates neither FI nor CO-PA. Documents with billing errors are recorded in transaction VFX3 (release billing documents to accounting). These errors need to be corrected and the billing document should be posted to FI and CO-PA using RELEASE TO ACCOUNTING. This function creates the FI document, as well as the line item in CO-PA.

Matching the cost of goods sold and revenue

 Billing errors recorded in transaction VFX3 (release billing documents to accounting) should be monitored periodically — at the minimum at period end — in order to keep FI and CO-PA reconciled from a matching cost and revenue standpoint.

When billing document data is posted, the online transfer function transfers the values directly into profitability analysis.

Valuation using material cost estimates determines the cost of sales when a sales transaction is posted to CO-PA. Quantities of products sold are multiplied by the standard costs of goods manufactured, thereby including detailed fixed and variable cost components for the cost of goods manufactured in the individual contribution margins.

Costing valuation is performed by using a cost estimate, which is online and in real time through the valuation strategy (product costing process), at the time the billing document flows into FI.

Figure 11.6 shows characteristics posted for a CO-PA document generated at the time of billing, while Figure 11.7 depicts value fields posted to CO-PA.

The menu path is as follows: ACCOUNTING • CONTROLLING • PROFITABILITY ACTUAL POSTINGS • DISPLAY LINE ITEMS.

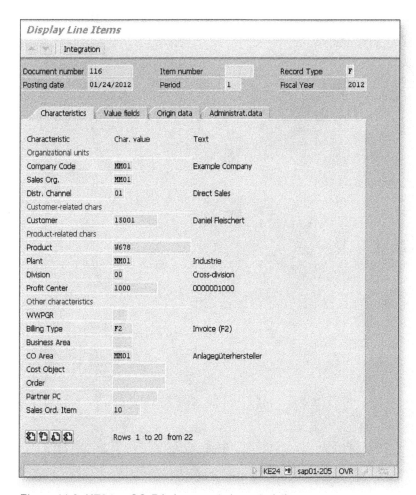

Figure 11.6: KE24 — CO-PA document characteristics

171

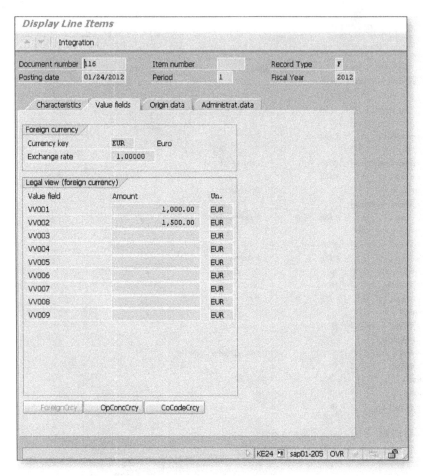

Figure 11.7: KE24 — CO-PA document value fields

11.5 Flow of actual values from FI and CO

Data can be transferred to CO-PA from FI through a manual journal entry, or through certain automatic entries from MM, such as physical inventory differences, material revaluations, etc.

CO-PA allows the assignment of fixed costs and the excess costs in production to profitability segments. The over-absorption/under-absorption remaining for the production cost centers are transferred periodically to CO-PA through *assessments*. Additionally, costs can also be transferred from administrative cost centers to CO-PA.

PA transfer structure allows mapping of such costs to value fields. Transaction KEI1 is used to map such cost elements (or a group of cost elements) to a specific value field.

Figure 11.8 depicts transaction KECM (CO-PA: Customizing Monitor) where several cost elements (listed below) are mapped to value field VV365 (price differences).

231520 — Loss of price difference from lower levels

232500 — Loss from revaluation of own materials

281520 — Gain of price difference from lower levels

282500 — Gain from revaluation of own materials

Actual amounts posted to these four cost elements will flow to one single value field, VV365.

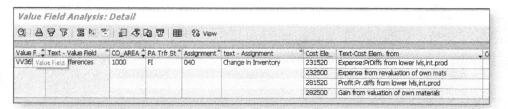

Value Field Analysis: Detail								
Value F...	Text - Value Field	CO_AREA	PA Trfr St	Assignment	text - Assignment	Cost Ele...	Text-Cost Elem. from	C
VV365	Value Field fferences	1000	FI	040	Change in Inventory	231520	Expense:PrDiffs from lower lvls,int.prod	
						232500	Expense from revaluation of own mats	
						281520	Profit:Pr.diffs from lower lvls,int.prod	
						282500	Gain from valuation of own materials	

Figure 11.8: KECM — PA transfer structure with several cost elements mapped to one value field

11.6   Flow of actual values during settlement

Production variances for cost objects are transferred to CO-PA when process/production orders are settled; such variances are transferred to display the individual variance categories in CO-PA.

The system allows mapping one cost element to several value fields depending on the type of variance category. As shown in Figure 11.9, different value fields (VV290, VV300, VV320, VV330, VV340, VV350, VV360, and VV360) are mapped for a single cost element (400000 – Consumption of Raw Material) depending on the type of variance category (PRIV, QTYV, LSFV, RSUV, INPV, SCRP, OPPV and REMV).

However, if the variances are not required to be broken down with this level of detail, then they can be mapped to a single value field, production variances.

Value Fiel	Text - Value Field	CO_AREA	PA Trfr St	Assignments	text - Assignment	Cost El	Text-Cost Elem. from	VCat	Text - Variance Cat.
VV290	Price variance	1000	C1	020	Price variance	400000	Consumption, raw material 1	PRIV	Input Price Variance
VV300	Quant. Variance Mat.	1000	C1	030	Quantity variances material		Consumption, raw material 1	QTYV	Input Quantity Variance
VV320	Lot-size Variance	1000	C1	060	Lot size variances		Consumption, raw material 1	LSFV	Lot Size Variance/Fixe
VV330	Usage variance	1000	C1	040	Resource usage variance		Consumption, raw material 1	RSUV	Resource-Usage Varian
VV340	Input Variances	1000	C1	050	Input variance		Consumption, raw material 1	INPV	Remaining Input Varia
VV350	Scrap	1000	C1	010	Scrap		Consumption, raw material 1	SCRP	Scrap
VV360	Remaining Variances	1000	C1	065	Output price variance		Consumption, raw material 1	OPPV	Output Price Variance
VV360	Remaining Variances	1000	C1	070	Remaining variance		Consumption, raw material 1	REMV	Remaining Variance
VV290	Price variance	1000	C1	020	Price variance	400001	Ext. procured material scrapped	PRIV	Input Price Variance
VV320	Lot-size Variance	1000	C1	060	Lot size variances		Ext. procured material scrapped	LSFV	Lot Size Variance/Fixe
VV330	Usage variance	1000	C1	040	Resource usage variance		Ext. procured material scrapped	RSUV	Resource-Usage Varian
VV340	Input Variances	1000	C1	050	Input variance		Ext. procured material scrapped	INPV	Remaining Input Varia
VV350	Scrap	1000	C1	010	Scrap		Ext. procured material scrapped	SCRP	Scrap
VV360	Remaining Variances	1000	C1	065	Output price variance		Ext. procured material scrapped	OPPV	Output Price Variance
VV360	Remaining Variances	1000	C1	070	Remaining variance		Ext. procured material scrapped	REMV	Remaining Variance
VV290	Price variance	1000	C1	020	Price variance	400002	Quality control cons., external material	PRIV	Input Price Variance
VV300	Quant. Variance Mat.	1000	C1	030	Quantity variances material		Quality control cons., external material	QTYV	Input Quantity Variance
VV320	Lot-size Variance	1000	C1	060	Lot size variances		Quality control cons., external material	LSFV	Lot Size Variance/Fixe
VV330	Usage variance	1000	C1	040	Resource usage variance		Quality control cons., external material	RSUV	Resource-Usage Varian
VV340	Input Variances	1000	C1	050	Input variance		Quality control cons., external material	INPV	Remaining Input Varia
VV350	Scrap	1000	C1	010	Scrap		Quality control cons., external material	SCRP	Scrap
VV360	Remaining Variances	1000	C1	065	Output price variance		Quality control cons., external material	OPPV	Output Price Variance
VV360	Remaining Variances	1000	C1	070	Remaining variance		Quality control cons., external material	REMV	Remaining Variance

Figure 11.9: KECM — PA transfer structure with variance categories with one cost element mapped to several value fields

11.7 Conclusion

CO-PA provides the data transfer and valuation of sales documents and FI/MM documents for relevant market dimensions.

In addition, CO-PA also offers a full range of allocation transactions that enable the application of overhead costs to the products, customers, and divisions that incurred them.

"So what we have seen up until now," Erin said, "is that CO-PA is a very powerful tool for finding out whether we are making any money or not. Corporate has information on gross sales, promotional discounts, returns, cost of goods sold, and fixed costs. They have analyzed this information for our new product line. Even though the sales and costs are in line with the expectations, the discounts are what seem to be creating noise."

"But what about fixed costs?" Carl asked. "Our fixed costs are the same as last year. We have not added any capacity to manufacture this new product line, we just switched three lines from the old product line."

"You bring up a good point," Alex said. "Fixed costs remain fixed for the most part. Could it be that the promotional discounts are temporary in nature and if we remove them from the mix the line will be profitable? Maybe our volumes were low given the initial launch and we may have an uptick in the coming months?"

"Bravo, Alex!" Bob said. "I did not think of that. I remember corporate telling me that they are checking with marketing on how long the promotion lasts. They spoke about having sought some special approvals and funding for this promotion, so I think this is temporary in nature. Let me ask if they have an update. I will go to my office and make few phone calls. Alex and Erin, can I ask you to review the data for the last week in the meantime? Maybe the promotions are already phased out now? Maybe corporate has looked at the last completed month in the system, but not the latest data. Everything is real time, so we should be able to verify quickly."

Alex and Erin looked up data from last week and did find that promotions did not show up on the billing documents or CO-PA documents. Bob received a similar feedback from corporate and marketing. Additionally, marketing stated that the new product line had been well received in the market and the volumes were likely to go up in the next few months. The new product line was making money after all; it was only a short-term discount and low volumes that were skewing the numbers.

"Well, great job team," Bob said. "Thanks to the details captured in the system, we were able to put our heads together and analyze what was going on. Carl, it looks like you are locked in on those three production lines for not eight, but the next twenty weeks! Let us all celebrate. Lunch is on me!" Bob thanked everyone. Everyone had a sense of achievement at the end of this long meeting.

12 "The numbers should match!" A controller's dream...

"Only accountants can save the world — through peace, goodwill and reconciliations."
— the alternative accountant

"Hey, Alex, I need your help." Dave, the inventory controller at the Chocotown facility spoke at a fast pace as he walked hurriedly into Alex's office one afternoon. "I have an e-mail from the supply chain lead at headquarters stating that the inventory numbers for the last month are off. I believe the numbers I reported are accurate and were pulled based on the same method that we have consistently used for months. I am not sure what is going on!"

"They may not be looking at the numbers correctly," Alex said. "Bob and I reviewed the numbers in our monthly report. Let's ask Erin if she can help solve this puzzle. I wanted to ask her a few questions about MM-FI integration anyway."

12.1 MB5L: List of stock values

"I have seen this in the past," Erin said. "We had a similar issue several months back. Likely, the folks at HQ are using MB5L with the wrong selection parameters."

"MB5L? Never heard of this transaction," Dave said.

"Me neither!" Alex said.

"Okay, let's go step by step," Erin said. "Tell me, Dave, what do you use to view your current inventory?"

12.2 MMBE: Stock overview

"MMBE for an individual material and MB52 for multiple materials or entire plant," Dave said. "Here, let me show you."

Dave opened his laptop and showed two transactions to Erin and Alex.

Figure 12.1 displayed the MMBE STOCK OVERVIEW screen for an individual material.

The menu path is as follows: LOGISTICS • MATERIALS MANAGEMENT • INVENTORY MANAGEMENT • ENVIRONMENT • STOCK • STOCK OVERVIEW.

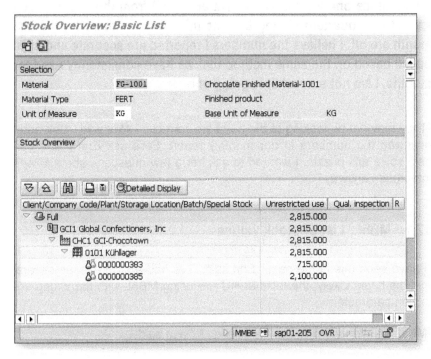

Figure 12.1: MMBE — Inventory snapshot for an individual material

12.3   MB52: Warehouse stock of material

"Now let me show you MB52 that I use for all my materials. I even have a layout set up so that I get to see those columns that I use most often."

Dave proudly showed the MB52 selection screen that he was so familiar with (see Figure 12.2).

The menu path is as follows: LOGISTICS • MATERIALS MANAGEMENT • INVENTORY MANAGEMENT • ENVIRONMENT • STOCK • WAREHOUSE STOCK.

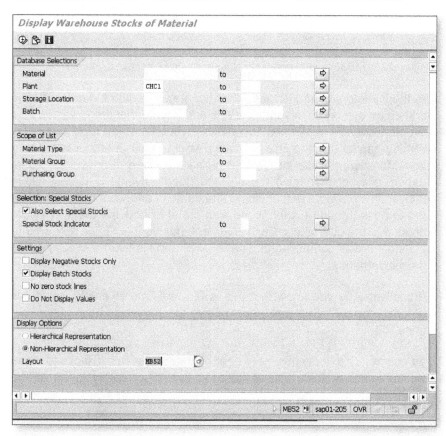

Figure 12.2: MB52 — Inventory snapshot for multiple materials (selection)

Once Dave clicked ⊕ execute on the top left corner, a nice report showed the current inventory levels for each of the materials with batch numbers. It even showed the amount of inventory held in the plant. Figure 12.3 shows the MB52 output screen.

Material	Material Description	Plnt	Name 1	MTyp	SLoc	S	Batch	BUn	Unrestr.	Crcy	Value Unre	Trans./Tfr	Val. in Tr	Qual.Insp.	Value in Q
FG-1001	Chocolate Finished Material-1001	CHC1	GCI-Chocotown	FERT	0101		0000000383	KG	715	USD	3,201.77	0	0.00	0	0.00
FG-1001	Chocolate Finished Material-1001	CHC1	GCI-Chocotown	FERT	0101		0000000384	KG	0	USD	0.00	0	0.00	0	0.00
FG-1001	Chocolate Finished Material-1001	CHC1	GCI-Chocotown	FERT	0101		0000000385	KG	2,100	USD	9,403.80	0	0.00	0	0.00
RAW-1001	Chocolate Raw Material-1001	CHC1	GCI-Chocotown	ROH	0001		1	G	7,150,000	USD	21,450.00	0	0.00	0	0.00
*										USD	34,055.57		0.00		0.00

MB52 ⋅ sap01-205 OVR

Figure 12.3: MB52 — Inventory snapshot for multiple materials (output)

As the inventory controller of GCI's Chocotown facility, it was Dave's job to keep an eye on the inventory levels and ensure that there was optimal inventory for raw materials. Too much inventory would lock in a lot of working capital and too little inventory would result in production downtime. Moreover, for the last two years, he had been given the additional responsibility of managing the finished goods inventory as well. Dave enjoyed this new role and anything that came in and went out of the plant had to pass through his team. He was proud of how the team was contributing to the operations. Each shipment that went out to be delivered to a customer was something that gave Dave and his team a special sense of achievement.

"Excellent! And you know that this is the real-time inventory, as of this moment, correct?" Erin was leading Dave to what would have played out at the HQ.

"Of course. This is my inventory right now as we speak. Thanks to these two transactions, I am able to keep an eye on inventory levels all the time."

12.4   MB51: Material document list

"Good! So can you tell me what the inventory was on the last day of the previous period?" Erin said.

"Well, I could give you the number provided there were no movements since then!" Dave said. "Jokes aside, as we know, this plant runs seven days a week and there are material movements all the time and the inventory levels keep changing all the time! What I can do is take the current inventory level from MB52, back out all the transactions that took place from first of the month through today from MB51 and give you the inventory as of the last day of the prior month."

The menu path is as follows: LOGISTICS • MATERIALS MANAGEMENT • IN-VENTORY MANAGEMENT • ENVIRONMENT • LIST DISPLAYS • MATERIAL DOCU-MENTS.

"Good idea, Dave," Erin said. "The MB51 material document list will provide all the movements for a given date range and you can adjust MB52 as of now to get to the answer, but I do not think that will be necessary. Let me show you another way to do it."

Erin showed a screen from her machine to Alex and Dave.

"MB5L is the general ledger report for MB52. The headquarters team uses this report to tie the inventory number in materials management to the inventory number in the general ledger. Look at the selection screen."

Erin showed Figure 12.4 to Alex and Dave. "Pay attention to the period selection button. I have selected CURRENT PERIOD in the report."

The menu path is as follows: LOGISTICS • MATERIALS MANAGEMENT • IN-VENTORY MANAGEMENT • PERIODIC PROCESSING • LIST OF STOCK VALUES.

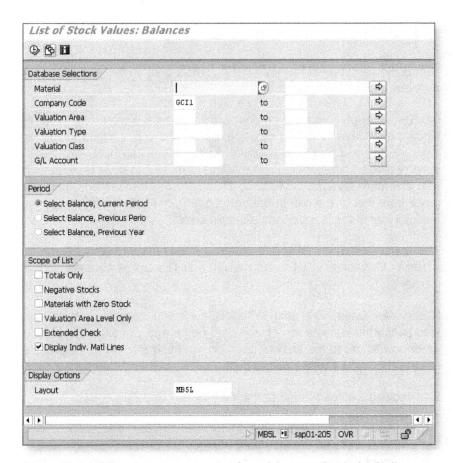

Figure 12.4: MB5L — Inventory snapshot financial accounting (selection)

Erin ran the report to get the output in the next screen (see Figure 12.5). "As you can see, the inventory value for current period in MB5L will tie to the number reported in MB52."

Figure 12.5: MB5L — Inventory snapshot financial accounting current period (output)

"And it does!" exclaimed Dave. "Also, I do not see the batch number and storage location here. So to me, I would still go by my good old MB52 that captures both storage location, as well as batch number."

"You are absolutely correct, Dave. MB5L does not have as much detail as MB52 and therefore, you should continue to use MB52 for your purposes," Erin said.

"To me, MB5L looks like an accountant's report for inventory," Alex said. "Additionally, we are also able to see the inventory balance by GL account, which basically means that this information is available in real time."

"But, how do we explain what headquarters is looking at?" Dave said.

"Yes, let's try to clarify," Erin said. "Let me show you how MB5L will change if I ran it for the previous period."

She went back to the MB5L selection screen, changed the selection to PREVIOUS PERIOD and ran the report again (see Figure 12.6). "As you will see, there was no change in the raw material. However, finished material changed a bit." Erin pointed to material FG-1001.

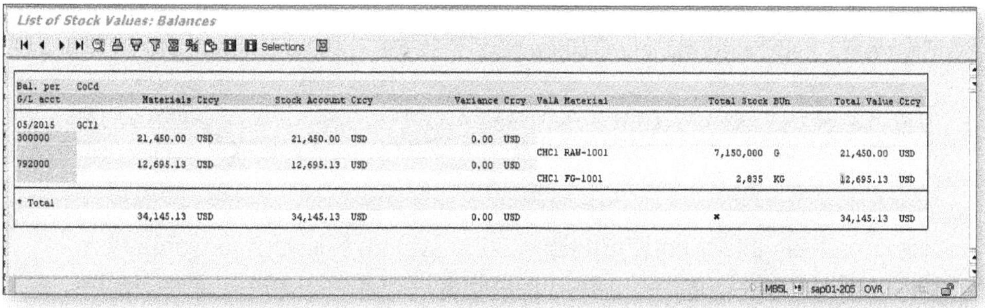

Figure 12.6: MB5L — Inventory snapshot in financial accounting for previous period (output)

"Dave, can you run MB51 and see what movements took place for FG-1001 since the beginning of the month?" Erin asked.

"Yes, we sold about 20 KG. We did not produce anything this month yet. Given that my current inventory is 2,815 KG, I would say we had an inventory of 2,835 KG at the end of last month," Dave explained.

"Exactly. And look at what MB5L is showing you for the previous period—2,835 KG!" Erin exclaimed.

"Wow. This is neat!" Dave said. "But do I need to run both MB52 and MB51 for every material?"

"No, I have another transaction for that," Erin said. "Try running MB5B through the last day of the month. Let's do it together." Erin went to MB5B in her system.

12.5 MB5B: Stock on posting date

"As you will see from the initial selection, MB5B is run for a given date range. You want to know what the stock is at the end of the last month, so you should run it from the beginning of the month to the end of the prior month. Let me run it for the beginning of the year just to demonstrate."

Figure 12.7 showed the initial selection of MB5B.

The menu path is as follows: LOGISTICS • MATERIALS MANAGEMENT • INVENTORY MANAGEMENT • ENVIRONMENT • STOCK • STOCK FOR A POSTING DATE.

"Now, as I run this report," Erin said, "the system will work forwards from the start date and consider all movements that took place to give us the quantity and value of inventory as at the given posting date."

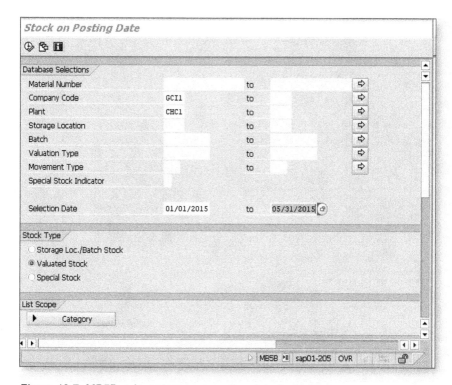

Figure 12.7: MB5B— Inventory on a posting date (selection)

"Oh, so it works forwards, whereas my approach of MB52 and MB51 combined is more of a backwards calculation," Dave said.

"Precisely!" Erin said. "As you will see in the MB5B output (see Figure 12.8), it shows us opening inventory, receipts, issues, and finally the closing inventory. And there is our 2,835 KG of FG-1001!"

"That is nice," Dave said. "At least I do not have to run two reports and manually calculate the numbers."

Material Stocks Between 01/01/2015 and 05/31/2015

| ◄◄ ◄ ► ►◄ ⊠ ‰ ⬚ ⎙ ⬚ ⬚ ⬚ |

Valuation Area   CHC1
Material   FG-1001
Description   Chocolate Finished Material-1001

Stock/Value on 01/01/2015	0	KG		0.00	USD
Total/Val. of Receipts	3,230	KG		14,581.54	USD
Total/Value of Issues	395-	KG		1,886.41-	USD
Stock/Value on 05/31/2015	2,835	KG		12,695.13	USD

SLoc	MvT	S	Mat. Doc.	Item	DocumentNo	Pstng Date		Quantity	BUn	Amount in LC
0101	101		5000020000	1	5000000000	03/23/2015		1,050	KG	4,819.50
			5000020022		4800000000	04/11/2015		0	KG	117.60-
0101	101		5000020022	1	5000000002	04/11/2015		2,100	KG	9,403.80
0101	201		4900008140	1	4900000004	04/30/2015		200-	KG	895.60-
0101	551		4900008141	1	4900000005	04/30/2015		50-	KG	223.90-
0101	202		4900008142	1	4900000006	04/30/2015		80	KG	358.24
0101	201		4900008143	1	4900000007	04/30/2015		145-	KG	649.31-
*								2,835	KG	12,695.13

Valuation Area   CHC1
Material   RAW-1001
Description   Chocolate Raw Material-1001

Stock/Value on 01/01/2015	0	G		0.00	USD
Total/Val. of Receipts	11,900,000	G		35,700.00	USD
Total/Value of Issues	4,750,000-	G		14,250.00-	USD
Stock/Value on 05/31/2015	7,150,000	G		21,450.00	USD

SLoc	MvT	S	Mat. Doc.	Item	DocumentNo	Pstng Date		Quantity	BUn	Amount in LC
0001	561		4900008100	1	4900000000	03/23/2015		10,000,000	G	30,000.00
0001	261		4900008101	1	4900000001	03/23/2015		950,000-	G	2,850.00-
0001	261		4900008124	1	4900000002	04/11/2015		1,900,000-	G	5,700.00-
0001	262		4900008125	1	5000000001	04/11/2015		1,900,000	G	5,700.00
0001	261		4900008126	1	4900000003	04/11/2015		1,900,000-	G	5,700.00-
*								7,150,000	G	21,450.00

| ▷ MB5B ▣ sap01-205 OVR |

Figure 12.8: MB5B — Inventory on a posting date (output)

Alex could sense what may have made headquarters think that the inventory numbers were off. He proposed a hypothesis to Erin and Dave. "Could it be that the MB5L report had the incorrect selection, leading headquarters to conclude that we were off?"

"You are on the money, Alex!" Erin said. "This is what happened last time, too. You see, MB5L has the company code as well as valuation area (the plant) in the initial selection. Even though the valuation area is in the selection, I do not recommend that you input the plant in the initial screen. You can always subtotal or filter it in the output screen. The same rule applies to all fields below the company code level."

MB5L selection

It is not best practice to run transaction MB5L (list of stock values) below the company code level because restrictions on these fields, such as material and/or valuation area, can lead to incorrect results.

"Got it!" Dave said. "So someone in headquarters put our plant CHC1 in the selection and got an incorrect result. Given that our company code GCI1 includes additional plants in the group, the numbers did not tie to what we reported last month. They should ideally run it for GCI1 and then subtotal it for CHC1 to get the number for our plant."

"Absolutely!" Erin said. "Do you want to clarify this observation with headquarters and see if this is what occurred?"

"Sure, let me call them from my office and I will get back to you folks shortly," Dave said.

"So what do you think, Alex?"

12.6 OBYC: MM-FI account determination

"It makes sense to me," Alex said. "Thanks for providing an explanation to the issue. I do have a question about various movement types though. I was going through MB51 the other day and noticed each material had different types of movements and each movement had a different accounting flow. Can you provide me an overview of movement types please?"

"Sure," Erin said. "It may be a bit on the technical side, but you seem to be interested in understanding the technical setup. Once you understand this setup, you will be able to visualize the flow and navigate through the system efficiently. In fact, transaction OBYC *MM-FI account determination* forms the core of SAP's integration between these two modules. Thanks to this tight integration, all these materials management reports that we saw MMBE, MB52, MB5B, and MB51 reflect accurately in financial accounting reports like MB5L. Look at this chart." Erin pointed Alex to Figure 12.9 which addressed movement types and accounting entries.

The menu path is as follows: TOOLS • CUSTOMIZING • IMG • SPRO EXE-
CUTE PROJECT • MATERIALS MANAGEMENT • VALUATION AND ACCOUNT AS-
SIGNMENT • ACCOUNT DETERMINATION • ACCOUNT DETERMINATION WITHOUT
WIZARD • CONFIGURE AUTOMATIC POSTINGS • ACCOUNT ASSIGNMENT.

Process	Movement Type - Description	Transaction-Account Modifier	Debit GL	Debit GL Description	Transaction-Account Modifier	Credit GL	Credit GL Description
Purchase of Raw Material	101 - Goods receipt for Purchase Order	BSX	300000	Inventory - Raw Material	WRX	191100	Goods Received / Invoice Received
Consumption of Raw Materials to Process Order	261 - Goods issue for order	GBB-VBR	400010	Raw materials consumed	BSX	300000	Inventory - Raw Material
Production of Semi-Finished Materials for Process Order	101 - Goods receipt for Process Order	BSX	790000	Unfinished products	GBB-AUF	895000	Factory output of production orders
Consumption of Semi-Finished Materials to Process Order	261 - Goods issue for order	GBB-VBR	890000	Semi-finished products consumed	BSX	790000	Unfinished products
Production of Finished Materials for Process Order	101 - Goods receipt for Process Order	BSX	792000	Finished goods inventory	GBB-AUF	895000	Factory output of production orders
Sampling for Quality Inspection	331 - Goods issue to sampling Quality Inspection	GBB-VQP	237000	Losses - consumption of quality control	BSX	792000	Finished goods inventory
Sale of Finished Material	601 - Goods issue: delivery	GBB-VAX	892000	Change in finished products inventory	BSX	792000	Finished goods inventory
Scrapping of Finished Material	551 - Goods issue for scrapping	GBB-VNG	890001	Scrapped material - own production	BSX	792000	Finished goods inventory
Cycle Count (Physical Inventory) of Finished Material	701 - Goods receipt for physical inventory adjustment	BSX	792000	Finished goods inventory	GBB-INV	233000	Losses - Inventory variance
Initial Inventory Load of Finished Material	561 - Initial entry of stock balances	BSX	792000	Finished goods inventory	GBB-BSA	799999	Inventory migration
Consumption of Raw Material from Sub-Contractor stock (special stock "O")	543 - Goods issue from stock at sub-contractor	GBB-VBO	400010	Raw materials consumed	BSX	300000	Inventory - Raw Material
Production of Finished Goods by Sub-Contractor (Production)	101 - Goods receipt from sub-contractor	BSX	792000	Finished goods inventory	BSV	893010	Sub-contract stock change
Production of Finished Goods by Sub-Contractor (Tolling Fee)	101 - Goods receipt from sub-contractor	FRL	417001	Purchased services	WRX	191100	Goods Rcvd/Invoice Rcvd

Figure 12.9: Movement types and accounting entries

"As you can see," Erin said, "we have the process listed in the column
furthest to the left, with movement type in the next column, and the debit
and credit posting in the subsequent columns. You will also find the
transaction and *account modifier*. These are SAP's terms for logically
grouping similar types of transactions. The transaction-account modifier,
along with the *valuation class* drive the accounting entries. Let me give
you an example."

"You may have seen an accounting entry at the time of purchase of raw
material as a debit to inventory and credit GR/IR," Erin said. "Well, the
configuration setup of transaction BSX (inventory posting) is responsible
for the inventory posting and WRX (GR/IR clearing account) for GR/IR
posting. So when movement type 101 is used to record goods receipt of
raw material (valuation class 3000) for a purchase order, the system
looks up the GL account for transaction BSX and WRX for valuation
class 3000 and records in the accounting document.

Transaction keys and account modifier

 Transaction keys are used to determine general ledger accounts used by the system. Account modifier is used to differentiate account determination depending on the procedure.

The transaction key is predefined in the SAP system and cannot be changed. The transaction-account modifier and the valuation class drive the accounting entries.

The transaction key in MM-FI account determination is not the same as transaction code. A transaction code is an alphanumeric code that represents a particular task in SAP. It allows users to access tasks directly without having to use menu paths.

"Similarly, when this raw material is consumed using movement type 261, the system looks up transaction GBB (offsetting entry for inventory posting) for account modifier (consumption for internal goods issues) and that reflects the GL account in the accounting document.

"The OBYC MM-FI account determination configuration is set up at the time of original implementation and once set up, these accounts are derived behind the scenes. Of course, you want to test the setup before going live to ensure that the correct accounts are being hit for the respective transactions. You can change this configuration after go-live, but the revised setup needs to be thoroughly tested, otherwise we may run the risk of impacting regular operations."

"Thank you for the explanation Erin. I understand now," Alex said. "The other day I had an audit query where the auditors wanted me to provide GL postings for all samples consumed for quality inspection for one of our finished materials. I looked things up and saw that every material document that had movement type 331 had the same accounting impact. Now I know that the system was using GBB-VQP and BSX for the posting."

"Erin, Alex—you were both right!" Dave said as he walked in to Erin's office. "Headquarters was using valuation area in the selection. I asked them to re-run the report at company code level and they were able to get to the same inventory number that we reported. Thanks for all of your help."

12.7 Conclusion

"Anytime, Dave," Erin said. "What I have always learned is that the system always behaves the right way. We just need to know where to look. Many times, someone may have performed a transaction incorrectly, or may have run a report incorrectly. What do you say, Alex?"

"I agree," Alex said. "I have always learned a lot when I go with the approach *it is always the people and process that break things, the system always works correctly!*"

13 Conclusion—What if we acquired a company?

"Alex, did you read the news on intranet?" Bob asked to Alex one day. "We are acquiring another confectionery company called National Confectioners, Limited (NCL). Headquarters is seeking suggestions on how to integrate them from an operations and IT standpoint. I know by now you have a good understanding of our system setup, so can you and Erin put something together so that we can present a case to management? I will introduce both of you to Frank, who is the plant controller at NCL. He will help you explain the setup at NCL so that you have all the facts."

"Sure, Bob, it will be my pleasure to work on this assignment," Alex said.

After a few days, Alex met with Bob. "This is what Erin and I suggest based on our discussions with Frank," Alex said. "NCL currently uses a home-grown system for their day-to-day operations. We recommend that we bring them over to our SAP system in order to leverage our system setup and harmonize our processes."

- ▶ **Company code**—NCL will be set up as a separate company code. Management would like to maintain NCL as an independent entity, while leveraging the reach of GCI's distribution network.

- ▶ **Chart of accounts**—We will continue to use the existing chart of accounts. This will facilitate consolidation of reporting of all our company codes. We will simply need to extend GL accounts to NCL company code.

- ▶ **Operating concern, fiscal year variant, and controlling area**—We recommend that NCL use GCI's operating concern, fiscal year variant, and controlling area given that the management wants a single internal reporting view of combined operations of GCI and NCL.

- **Plants** — NCL's three manufacturing facilities will be set up as three separate plants, assigned to the new company code for NCL. There is already a lot of goods movement between the three plants. We envisage a lot of movement between GCI's plants and NCL's plants, this will be enabled using intercompany stock transfer.

- **Sales** — NCL currently uses the distribution network of another company. They will switch over to GCI's distribution network. This will allow the combined company to use GCI's sales and distribution setup.

- **Profit centers and cost centers** — We need to set up new profit centers and cost centers for NCL. NCL's manufacturing facilities will be depicted in the profit center hierarchy and cost center hierarchy, similar to GCI's current setup.

- **Activity type** — GCI's current cost drivers are direct labor and machine hours. NCL uses an additional cost driver for machine setup cost. This is a substantial cost component for NCL and they would like to continue to have this visibility when they move over to our system. We may plan on implementing this additional activity type at GCI as well. However, we need to review the efforts involved in retrofitting GCI's recipes by production planning team.

- **Cost allocations** — Apart from the plant-specific cost allocations to replicate GCI's structure in NCL, we will also need HQ cost allocations to NCL.

- **Internal orders** — Since integration of NCL into GCI requires significant investment over the next eighteen months or so, we recommend using internal orders for each specific function so that management is able to allocate budgets and track actual costs.

- **Material master** — There are lot of common raw materials between GCI and NCL that we should extend to NCL's plants. New material masters will be required for finished materials given that we have very few common finished products.

- **Manufacturing processes** — NCL currently uses production orders in their internal system. They do not use PI sheets. We plan to implement process orders for NCL, this will allow harmonization of processes and also provide benefit of using PI sheet.

▶ **R&D costs** — NCL has a dedicated research and development setup and there is a need to track cost of process orders used for R&D. As we know, GCI does not have as much R&D. We currently issue goods to an R&D cost center. We propose using a new process order type for R&D purposes. Each R&D initiative will be created as a process order, to be settled to cost center.

"This is very good. I am pleased by the recommendations," Bob said. "This is exactly what headquarters is looking for. Thanks!"

Alex and Erin had put in a lot of effort into understanding NCL requirements from Frank. Alex was especially proud of having incorporated his learning into this special assignment.

Note to the reader: The SAP Controlling module consolidates the benefits of the integrated nature of the SAP software. Whereas processes in SAP Finance are very similar in most organizations, SAP Controlling offers some variety given that requirements differ from one company to another. Each client's SAP installation has its own design variants, but the overall goal is to provide management with visibility into the happenings in the organization.

As you may have noticed from the acquisition scenario, almost all the concepts that we looked at in the prior chapters were used in order to come up with the proposed design for integration of acquisition.

I hope you have enjoyed this exciting journey into this powerful tool!

You have finished the book.

A The Author

Ashish Sampat is a qualified finance and costing professional with nearly two decades of industry experience in the SAP Finance and Controlling space. Ashish has been an SAP consultant for most of his career with various consulting organizations and now works as an independent SAP FI/CO consultant. He has provided solutions in several areas of SAP Controlling including product costing, material ledger, and cost center accounting to global clients in consumer packaged goods, life sciences, and industrial sectors. Born and educated in India, Ashish now lives in suburban Chicago with his wife and two kids.

B Index

C Disclaimer

This publication contains references to the products of SAP SE.

SAP, R/3, SAP NetWeaver, Duet, PartnerEdge, ByDesign, SAP BusinessObjects Explorer, StreamWork, and other SAP products and services mentioned herein as well as their respective logos are trademarks or registered trademarks of SAP SE in Germany and other countries.

Business Objects and the Business Objects logo, BusinessObjects, Crystal Reports, Crystal Decisions, Web Intelligence, Xcelsius, and other Business Objects products and services mentioned herein as well as their respective logos are trademarks or registered trademarks of Business Objects Software Ltd. Business Objects is an SAP company.

Sybase and Adaptive Server, iAnywhere, Sybase 365, SQL Anywhere, and other Sybase products and services mentioned herein as well as their respective logos are trademarks or registered trademarks of Sybase, Inc. Sybase is an SAP company.

SAP SE is neither the author nor the publisher of this publication and is not responsible for its content. SAP Group shall not be liable for errors or omissions with respect to the materials. The only warranties for SAP Group products and services are those that are set forth in the express warranty statements accompanying such products and services, if any. Nothing herein should be construed as constituting an additional warranty.

More Espresso Tutorials Books

Sydnie McConnell & Martin Munzel:

First Steps in SAP® (2nd, extended edition)

▶ Learn what SAP and SAP software is all about!

▶ Enhanced with videos and audio comments

▶ Simple, consecutive examples

http://5045.espresso-tutorials.com

Martin Munzel:

New SAP® Controlling Planning Interface

▶ Introduction to Netweaver Business Client

▶ Flexible Planning Layouts

▶ Plan Data Upload from Excel

http://5011.espresso-tutorials.com

Michael Esser:

Investment Project Controlling with SAP®

▶ SAP ERP functionality for investment controlling

▶ Concepts, roles and different scenarios

▶ Effective planning and reporting

http://5008.espresso-tutorials.com

Stefan Eifler:

Quick Guide to SAP® CO-PA (Profitability Analysis)

► Basic organizational entities and master data
► Define the actual value flow
► Set up a planning environment
► Create your own reports

http://5018.espresso-tutorials.com

Paul Ovigele:

Reconciling SAP® CO-PA to the General Ledger

► Learn the Difference between Costing-based and Accounting-based CO-PA
► Walk through Various Value Flows into CO-PA
► Match the Cost-of-Sales Account with Corresponding Value Fields in CO-PA

http://5040.espresso-tutorials.com

Tanya Duncan:

Practical Guide to SAP® CO-PC (Product Cost Controlling)

► Cost Center Planning Process and Costing Run Execution
► Actual Cost Analysis & Reporting
► Controlling Master Data
► Month End Processes in Details

http://5064.espresso-tutorials.com

Janet Salmon & Ulrich Schlüter:

SAP® HANA for ERP Financials, 2nd edition

▶ Basic principles of SAP HANA

▶ The idea behind SAP Accounting powered by SAP HANA

▶ HANA applications in ERP Financials

▶ Implications on business processes

http://5092.espresso-tutorials.com

Ann Cacciottolli:

First Steps in SAP® Financial Accounting (FI)

▶ Overview of key SAP Financials functionality and SAP ERP integration

▶ Step-by-step guide to entering transactions

▶ SAP Financials reporting capabilities

▶ Hands-on instruction based on examples and screenshots

http://5095.espresso-tutorials.com